MW00571789

Published by **Polari Press**
www.polari.press @polaripress

ISBN 978-1-914237-11-9

Printed by Severn Print using vegetable
inks on Elements Fire 100gsm paper.
Typeset in 10/17 Roslindale.

Cover design and typesetting
by Peter Collins for Polari.

This second edition was printed in the UK
in May 2023.

Harsh Cravings

Jason Haaf

polari

This book is dedicated to my husband
and Mary MacLane

FOREWORD

IT'S A CHOICE to write this foreword as it's a choice to write this entire book. I suppose I'm writing to let you know that movement never stops, even if it feels stalled. In fact, I'm probably writing to remind myself of the same thing. My intentions are explanatory, as is my writing itself, but you'll see that soon enough. The people that I'll describe and the relationships I fear I don't bring justice to, have since evolved since I first brought my pen to paper.

My original aim that began in August 2020, a time of unrest and uncertainty, was to create a time capsule — and one that I've tried to not touch too much (although I don't take my own advice). My aim is to give you something unfiltered. I choose to record to make sense of it all; to make sense of the gray areas. Tonight though, as I write this, I feel like the shades I've provided may not be blended enough. I say that because it's only my voice you'll be reading and I understand the weight of that responsibility.

This foreword wouldn't be complete (which was really written out of a semi-neurotic need to always explain) without mentioning that much of everyday life has gone back to what you'd call normal in NYC (if there even is a normal anymore) since August 2020. I'm still figuring out what to do, how to navigate the present, what I'll go back to and what I'll move on from. My words are already a thing of the past and I wonder: are they clear; precise; accurate; maybe they're dramatic; do they expose too much; can I keep certain people from reading this; do they overreach; why share now; why this time; will I get myself in trouble; will I ever stop editing? I want to present myself to you, effectively, but I'm not glib enough to say that my expressions, my views, my interpretations are concrete and will not evolve with time. And time just keeps moving on and what you are about to read, it's already gone. And yet, here is where it is about to live, to be seen, by you.

Ever been inside your void?

AUGUST 2020

August 9, 2020
Brooklyn, New York
I don't think there is necessarily a right time to start recording. Now, though, with such stillness outside, now seems like an appropriate time.

I don't care to write a life story. Autobiographies, they're usually curated memories told in a straight line that are masturbatory to the one telling them.

What I care about is recording, to have a time stamp on my words, perhaps proof of who I was at the moment that this was written.

I've accepted that there is a competition in me that will not go away. There is a hunger within that I've given up on trying to dilute. Some things I can control, but for the most part I've stopped trying.

August 10

I suppose I should address that as I write this, we are in the middle of a pandemic. It has been five months since the United States has by large been on lock down, and I have been without a job since March. No, I don't look for things to do. I enjoy not working and not having to be alert for up to ten hours a day. I think of my past self, walking and perspiring at my job, exhausted and stalking/managing the lobby of Homecoming Hotel, a boutique hotel near Chelsea in Manhattan. And I wonder, who was that for?

Something though, shines through these times, through death, unrest, the unknown: the act of desire and my need to expose.

This appreciation I have for exposure goes back to 1989, when in grade school, a boy in my class would unzip his pants and show himself to me. I remember standing over him as his zipper came down. I have a memory of turning on him, telling the teacher what he'd done and hiding under a table while he was reprimanded. Or maybe I was the one hiding. Either way, intimacy is a tricky thing. I guess I've learned to not turn against it.

I consider myself sensitive and while I crave intimacy from others, I do not feel an immediate need to share my innermost fears to anyone who will listen, well, except to you and whoever else may read this.

I appreciate intimacy. If I were in a group setting, I would not be entertaining an audience of five to ten, but instead would be standing silently side-by-side with someone I want to be next to.

I like being silent, to look but not speak. No matter who you are, I will be quiet around you when we first meet. While I have a thirst for intimacy, my need for it is not soft or particularly friendly. It is watery and mercurial and it comes in blasts.

This thing—to be soft, Queer, and boastful of your platonic relationships, which seems to be such a trend these days—well, it doesn't quite work for me.

Aren't we led by desire? Is desire not the impetus for coming out of the proverbial closet? I stand aside and silence myself when I have these musings as they usually end in a rant, and I am fearful to offend. But I am not like everyone else, or the majority of the minority.

I have a fear of sounding like a hardened Gen X gay man. I don't identify with some of the habits of Gen Z, curating their personas while floating high in their idealism. Or am I, a Millennial, a romantic? And when did I, or we, start thinking of Gen X'ers as being hard? Weren't they the ones with their heads in the clouds, the romantics that the Baby Boomers thought of as lost and fleeting? Or was that the reputation of the white middle-class Boomers—before they were seduced by Ronald Reagan—flower power trading the good fight for a sweet and sedated suburban life?

August 11

Maybe it's the thrill of experiencing something for the first time that doesn't go away for me. Does it go away for anyone?

When the cases of Covid-19 started to fall in NY, I traveled upstate to spend a weekend with my friend Leo. Leo is a boisterous type. I've compared him to a grown-up version of one of the boys from the movie *The Sandlot*. He speaks loud at times with a thick Long Island accent. His hair, which he takes hair-thickening pills and shampoos for, is always covered by a backwards baseball cap. Leo grew up as the middle of four brothers, all similar in age, and he professes that he 'has a bit of bully in him.'

He moved to New Paltz, NY, in June, when he realized the pandemic was going to slow business for him in the city. It was a bold move, and I think a bright one. I saw, not long after he moved, that he was starved for company. I felt a certain hesitance when he invited me to stay the weekend with him. While the two of us had previously slept together, and Leo did have sex with my husband and I, I never slept over someone else's house, much less for a weekend.

Leo's proposition felt like a sleepover with a friend from grade-school who was having me over for the first time. His backward cap, loud mouth, and ever-present T-shirt and shorts only added to the feigned memory. It was sweet in its way, and something I wanted to do. My husband, Matthew, is an easy-going man and had no opposition to me going.

The day that Leo came to pick me up, I knew that he would park his car, ask to come inside, and use our bathroom before we left.

I said to Matthew, 'Watch, he's going to need to use the bathroom. He's that type.'

Minutes later, I received a text that said, 'I need to pee.'

After Leo took care of himself, Matthew kissed me goodbye and saw us off. I liked the feeling. I feel a sense of autonomy if and when I'm intimate with someone outside of my marriage. To have that exist openly, and to give in to all the emotions that it may bring, feels like freedom.

Shortly after arriving at Leo's, a quaint studio apartment overlooking a giant lake (or just a shallow, manmade body of water), we sat next to each other on his tan leather sofa. He picked up my legs and laid them on top of his own. The intertwining of legs between men is always an indicator of what is to come. He pinched the skin above my knee and his eyes looked glossed and hungry. We leaned into each other to kiss. He kisses messy, but not in a bad way. It's aggressive and open-mouthed and reminds me of the 6th grade. I ran my hand along the edge of his T-shirt. I'd been waiting to go beneath it and touch the hair peeking out of his collar.

'Take off your clothes,' he said.

I stripped completely down while he repositioned himself on the sofa. Fully dressed, he pulled his cock out through his zipper. I got on my knees and wrapped my mouth around his head. Leo had my phone in his hands and pressed Record.

When he laid me stomach-down on his bed and pushed into me, Leo was not a boy from *The Sandlot*. He was meaty, handsome, his chest and stomach blanketed in hair. He entered with force and he is aware of the force he uses, and he knows that it may shock. His force has made me squirm with discomfort, which likely encourages him. I looked back at him as he was pushing and pulling me by the waist. Around his neck dangled a thick, gold crucifix. He grabbed my chin, wrapped his other arm around my neck, and sloppily plunged his tongue into my open mouth.

That night, we curled up next to each other. The way we positioned ourselves, it felt very dominant and submissive, similar to our sex. But there was care there, a tenderness. We were not enveloped and entwined as if we were one because we are not one. There was though, for me, a gratitude for our exchange. Just under the tips of my skin, were little sparks like fireflies, brushing against the surface.

August 12

I would have liked to write about something today maybe say, abstract, but today, the whole day, I am only thinking about my job, if I have one, if I'm going to have insurance, if I need to reschedule a dental appointment, if I should refill my prescription while I'm insured, and how much this fucking hotel company I work for continues to keep fucking with me because upper management does not reach out and engage and let myself or others know if the business plans to remain open and if we have jobs.

The truth is, I haven't seen myself going back to Homecoming Hotel since we first closed in March due to the pandemic. Maybe it was the thousands of complaints that came to light, made by Black former employees, claiming racism and lack of acknowledgement, response, and leadership in the workplace as to why I don't see myself going back; I don't want to go back, I don't want to be a part of it. I don't want to be near lost promises of 'We'll do better,' and loose words meant to convey empathy and conviction.

One can only sweep so much dirt under a rug before it starts to show through the fabric.

I left the company once, but only for a short while. Before I left, I wrote a three page letter to the head of Human Resources. I expressed my grievances of feeling overworked, and of feeling like no one seemed to care that I was struggling. I could have spoken up before, but I was speaking up now. The real reason though, why I wrote the letter, was because earlier that week I found out that an Engineer refused to hang the Pride Flag in front of the building and made verbal comments about not wanting to do so and our Front Desk heard. I knew this was his homophobia, just as I knew of his racism, when an employee had approached me about the way he'd speak about Black people when they passed through the lobby. I was pissed, and I went past the General Manager and went straight to HR, and not HR for the property, but for the hotel group.

The General Manager, at the time, didn't like that I did this. He may have seen it as a dig that I didn't go to him first. I was conducting an interview in a downstairs office when I saw him approach the doorway. He was scrolling on his phone; news travels fast, and I knew he was reading the letter I had sent. After I wrapped up the interview, he motioned for me to go to an empty office, which was not his. I walked into the room with him, and he shut the door behind us. He sat down on a couch and crossed his legs.

'I'm reading through your letter here. And I'm reading, and reading, and reading. I'm waiting to see when the bottom is going to fall out,' he said.

I sat in the chair across from him, silent.

'Why didn't you come to me?' he asked.

'Honestly, because we've never really established any kind of relationship. I probably didn't feel comfortable knowing if I could.'

He stared at me, exhaled, resting his jaw between his thumb and index finger. 'I want you to know something about me. I change people's lives. People come to me, and I show them the way. You could have come to me, and I could have found where you needed to be. But now, now we're losing Jason Haas, a great employee.'

I didn't even correct him and remind him that my last name is *Haaf*.

I said, 'Look, I've been here a while, and I wrote the letter because I wanted my experience heard; I wanted to report what I knew, to have it be heard. And I think I got to a point where I didn't feel that I trusted enough to get my voice across anymore.'

He smiled at me. 'You remind me of my husband. If you eat a little spoonful of shit each time, you just keep taking it and taking it, and pretty soon, you'll be full of it. You have to step up, you have to use your voice.'

'Well, I mean, that's why I wrote that letter,' I said.

'You could have come to me. I would have taken care of this. I can tell that you don't let people take care of you. I could have helped you.'

The meeting was finished soon after that. I remember waiting for the elevator and smiling politely at the room attendants as they asked me how my day was. The head of the Housekeeping department must have known something was wrong and she met me in room 716, which I was supposed to be inspecting. She opened up the door and said, 'Jas?' with such a look of concern on her face. My breathing became heavier and I was trying so hard not to crack. Tears started welling into my eyes.

'Jas, Jas what's wrong?' she asked.

She walked towards me and put her hands on my shoulders and I melted under her care.

August 13

There is plenty that is unknown right now. I don't know what may happen day to day or what decisions may be made during this time that could affect my life and living. To relinquish this amount of control feels unnatural, but I assume one needs to give up their illusions of control and to just survive.

August 15

I dreamed of sex all night. I had two dreams, one involved a group of men, each one jacking off side-by-side in bed. That's when I entered, and climbed in with all of them.

I crave intimacy and I naturally crave having it with more people than just Matthew. While there is something extremely erotic of two (or more) strangers offering their dicks to each other, I prefer something to be behind it. Anonymous sex is fine and has its virtues. Yet, I have always taken to blurred lines and edges; a friendship with moments of romanticism; a comradery with cum. Desire alone, though, will not stand the test of time. That is what love is, which exceeds the erotic.

Weeks after meeting Matthew, I sat down on the R train, heading into Manhattan. I looked across the train cart and I saw this man, this stranger. He looked Italian and was at least 6'1.' His legs almost reached the middle of the aisle. He was hunched over, drawing something in a notebook. His brows were dark, chocolate brown, and his nose prominent and hooked. I was aware of the urge I felt to walk over and sit next to him, just to be near him.

When he glanced upward, our eyes met and I saw that it was Matthew. He smiled, walked towards me, and sat next to me.

'I didn't know that was you,' I said.

We met in the fall, six years ago, a season which has always offered a wave of calm.

August 16

Maybe desire should exist as its own island. Sometimes, we must visit that island, accept that we're stranded, and stay there for a few hours or days.

This morning I'm craving a scene between an aged man and youth. There is a ceremonial element at the thought of an older man acting as a father-figure delivering seed to his son. I wonder if this fantasy is both inevitable and collective among gay men. Although Matthew is my peer, my counterpart, he sometimes takes care of me like a father. He kisses me goodbye when he leaves the house, even if he's only gone for a few minutes. He cooks dinner for me almost every night and washes the dishes too. He provides support and service for me, as if I'm a child. Matthew could be a sibling taking care of their brother, or a father being dutiful towards his son. So, what does it mean, for roles to be so wrapped up and interchangeable? It means

I understand why David Cronenberg hits his audience over the head with Freudian symbols; it is inescapable.

I could call someone to come over right now, who is in fact the age of a father; much younger than mine of course, but a 20-year-old could easily be his son. His name is Rodrigo, and he's visiting the city from Woodstock for the weekend. We've not met in real life, though he does insist that he wants Matthew watching as he 'impregnates me'.

I do not invite him over, not yet.

August 18

The beginning of a relationship is a strange time and exploratory in a way. It is a time for unearthing. The first time Matthew and I had sex, I felt a surge of anger afterwords. An aggression began to course through me, and I went to the park and ran, with moments of fury. I was letting myself be affected, and there were many emotions; a feeling of relief, perhaps resentment that I did not have to fight against what I felt. I could lay on Matthew's chest, and he'd put his arm around me in a way that was soft and paternal. He did not grip me nor was his touch selfish; it was gentle and steadfast.

Six years later, he and I cannot know what one or the other does all the time. The other night, I heard what I thought was Matthew brushing his teeth in the bathroom. I thought the sound had such an odd rhythm, as if the motor was breaking. Then, I realized that it was not an electric toothbrush that I was hearing. Realizing it was a vibrator, my heart felt a certain pang. Matthew never really seemed interested in vibrators, at least using them on himself. I wondered if he was making a video to send to someone later.

My instinct was to let him know that I knew he was pleasuring himself and that it felt secretive. I fought the urge to let him know that he cannot hide from me. Then I thought, who am I to dictate what he can and cannot do, to his own body, in his own home and in his own privacy. He does not need to share everything he does with me. Still, I hated that feeling I had when he came out of the bathroom, minding his usual business. It felt like I was being lied to, or that the room was filled with a secret.

A few nights later, I heard the same noise coming from the bathroom. It turns out that vibrating hum, was in fact, not a vibrator at all. It was just Matthew, changing the speeds on his new electric razor.

August 19

What I need or crave, it cannot wait.

I do not trust that time is in my favor.

A new job, new cum, new body of work, new way of thinking, new attractions, new successes, new disappointments cannot wait. I must have them all, and I want them all right now.

The thing is, they all must wait because the United States and people and businesses and opportunity and travel are all barely moving.

Everything is barely moving.

August 20

I'm sitting under a tree at Greenwood Cemetery right now, which yes, sounds romantic. Isn't it all somewhat romantic: my yearning to have a closeness with men, to have a friend in adulthood that resembles a boyish adolescent friend, to have a quiet and caring father type near, to have a husband whom I can act like a child around. I wish I had a creative partner, someone who looks at me admirably, who wants me around for inspiration. The truth is, maybe I have all of these things, but it is the yearning for them that does not cease. Even if I obtain what I crave, there is still a phantom craving.

Moments ago, I passed a grave with a tombstone that read 'Woods.' A few seconds later, I passed a grave that read 'Williams.' And I am reminded of Will Woods.

Writing his name, Will Woods, hurls me back. Will Woods was... wretched is the first word that comes to mind. He was one of the most sexual men I've met, or at least he wanted me to believe. He appeared very scattered, and had one of the widest, toothiest, engaging smiles I'd seen.

Did I fall in love with him? Maybe.
Was it only lust? I'm not sure.

He told me he couldn't give me what I wanted, and that he was on a path of sexual, mental, perhaps spiritual exploration. Will could not find himself committed to anyone. He spoke of men and sexual encounters in such a detached, matter-of-fact way. I would have done almost anything to understand him. I did not want to be loved by him, not in the way of honor or fidelity. I wanted to be his source of want, of desire.

The closest I came to that was when we laid naked side by side, inside of a tent in Newburgh, NY, after a night of drinking. I had watched him build a fire, and he smelled of soap and burnt wood.

'I've wanted to do this all night,' he said.

Grabbing the back of my head, Will pushed his mouth onto mine. I may have been shaking as I thought, *I have him now*.

I did not have him, and I have never had Will Woods.

Will wanted someone naïve yet coy, someone willing but hesitant at the same time. Two years ago this month, he told me that he had fallen in love with a man in Paris, France. His new lover seemed to display all of the qualities listed above, and he was beautiful, tan, with thick brows and a chest covered in lush, black hair. Will forwarded me a letter that he had written to his newfound love. In it, he was asking, even begging his lover to open his legs for him, to let him inside and fuck him as deeply as he'd ever been fucked before. The letter read that Will was naked on his bed, mouth on his pillow, grinding himself into his mattress, imagining that he was inside of him. The funny thing is, when I opened up the letter, I thought it was my own. Why he gave me the letter to read, I don't know. It could have been his way of saying I long for him how you longed for me.

Will was rough, rough enough that I still see his name in quiet places.

August 21

A lot of gay men speak about not shaming desire, about being as free as they can be with their bodies.

Do they abide by their words?

A lot of gay artists draw dicks, the acts of fucking, fellatio, and threesomes.

Are they living their art?

There are a lot of Queer men who preach against monogamy, who say an open relationship is the way to go.

Have they ever been in one?

I hear a lot of men talk about their vulnerability.

Are they actually open?

August 22

I find myself intrigued that I live a domestic-esque life, even if it's not the most traditional. I'm surprised because a domestic life to me, while growing up, meant a lack of feeling. I secluded myself in my youth, to have minimal interactions with my parents. There was so much space, both literal and figurative. The house on 39th Court in Margate, Florida was always clean, always quiet. On Sunday afternoons, you would only hear the faint sounds of a game of golf, played at low volume on the television.

My bedroom was on the complete opposite side of the house as my parents. There was a dark hallway with empty bedrooms that I had to pass in order to reach my own. My parents never, ever shut their bedroom door. This led me to believe that there had to be an absence of sex. Neither of them were cold people. They both just traveled along their own orbit, and maybe I do too. We would occasionally pass each other throughout the house, but there were no dinner conversations and no family outings (not that I was overly eager to attend any). My mother, Carrie, would play the piano, one of her many short-lived hobbies. My dad would sunbathe for two to three hours every Sunday, deepening the red-brown color of his chest.

All of this quiet may have just been a sitting pot of boiling water, ready to spill over.

The remaining weeks of my parents living together, my mom, late one night, went into one of the vacant guest rooms where my father now slept.

'I'll put a bullet in your heart,' she told him as he lay in bed.

She was driven to the edge you could say, and he was calm as could be. Whatever he said back to her, it wasn't audible, because he had the power to always keep his voice steady and low-volume, especially when another person was breaking down.

Last night, I lay in my own bed with Matthew. The room was quiet, dark, hot with the A/C blasting. He kept looking at me with soft, intent eyes. What he was trying to say, I don't know. What his eyes say but his mouth never does, I cannot be sure. He lay his hand on my arm, and the room felt hotter. The blanket and Matthew's touch and warm body felt suffocating. I moved away from his hand touching me, and instantly, I felt regret.

In the morning, I apologized, and laid my head against his chest.

'It's okay, do you feel better now?' he asked.

'Yea.'

'I love you,' he said.

'I love you.'

August 23

Mary MacLane, whom this book is dedicated to, author of *I Await the Devil's Coming*, wrote about waiting. She waited for the Devil because he would provide her unbridled pleasure, an escape from the ordinary world around her.

I, too, wait for something to happen, for my heart to skip a beat.

I wait for something out of the ordinary to occur: *a possibility*. Something that will happen to me, that I don't have to pull from another galaxy, to bring into mine.

If the Devil showed up bearing a gift, I need to accept the gift that he delivers. There is no guarantee that another will come.

August 24

A man named Noah messaged me on Instagram yesterday. I never met Noah, but we'd been following each other on social media for a few months.

His posts have a gentleness to them. Most of them are pictures of his coworkers, or of animals, or a bike ride through nature.

'I live in Queens, you're in Brooklyn?' he asked.

I answered yes.

'Do you have a partner?'

'I do. His name is Matthew, we've been together for six years,' I said.

'Me too. Kort, two plus years. We're open.'

I already knew he was in a committed relationship judging from what I saw. There was a playful quality to Noah; he usually had his pet lizard perched on his shoulder. He looked like a granola-type with a mustache covering the top half of his lip. There were a couple shirtless pictures of him, and the roundness of his chest caught my attention. It was so broad, with blond hair around the nipples, and meaty muscle at its edges. I could tell that it had been more defined at one time. Now, there was weight on top of the muscle; soft over hard. I thought his body could be delightful to lay next to.

I wrote that I was free when he asked if I wanted to hang out. He said that he 'needed more friends, lol.' I couldn't tell how serious he was, but the fact that he mentioned it, I figured he might mean it.

'Maybe we could play a little if it goes there. I'm sorry to be so forward,' he wrote.

'No, I like it.'

Flirting with men online is like a plane taking off. Once there is the first suggestion of sex, the plane now lifts itself from the ground. Its wheels are safely tucked inside their compartments, and we are making our ascension.

I had visions of being outdoors with Noah, our partially clothed bodies pressed against each other. I told him this, and he suggested we go for a hike. He said he wanted to sniff me, kiss me, fuck me, and line my insides with his cum over and over again.

'I want to make you moan,' he wrote.

We sent each other real-time videos of us jacking off. Noah lifted his shirt, pinching his pink nipples while he stroked, showing off his pale, meaty chest. He told me

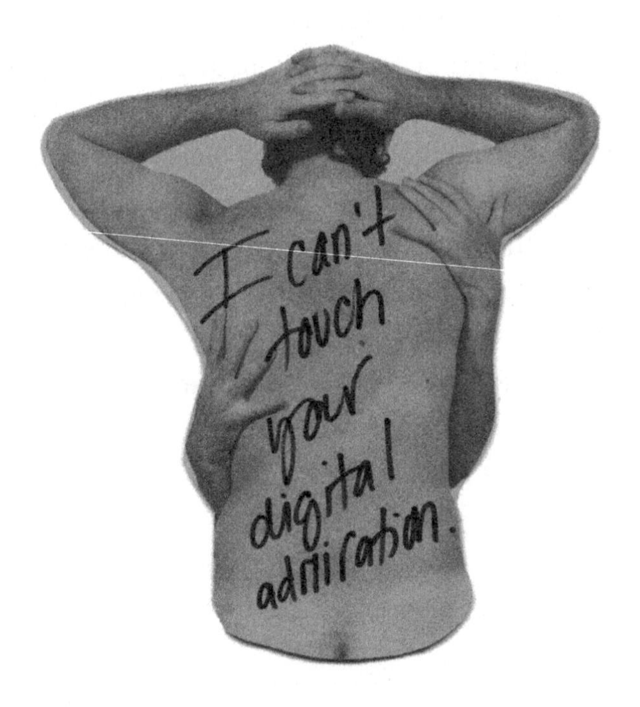

he was 'poz' and 'undetectable.' I wrote to him that I was 'negative and on PrEP.' It's interesting how the medical, and the sexual, and the need for a friend, and the need for a lover, and the need for connection, and the need for an escape merge together for gay men. I wonder if Noah will message me again. I imagine sitting next to him on a train on our way upstate. His palm faces upwards, ready to lead me into the woods.

August 25

I only came out twelve years ago, when I was 25. I'm not going to say, I had so many walls up, I wouldn't let anyone in. That's not my narrative. I think I've only wanted to let someone in, but would I let myself go?

The past is gone and I remind myself of that almost daily. Something, though, was crystallized twelve years ago. There may always be a crystallization of the time when a Queer person comes out.

I try not to think of it as the time that I was the most desired.

At 37, a sizable amount of experience and a life-partner later, I still feel at times like a 25-year-old virgin (which I was). God, twelve years wasn't even that long ago, and yet, in another ten, I'll be middle-aged.

What I remember most about 2008, was there being a tightness within myself: a concoction of fear, anxiety, cigarettes, an unknown future, being told to 'go with the flow.' I was not living the black-and-white 1960s French film, where I rolled around on white sheets with an ashtray on the bed scenario that I craved to be in. This was the real life of an uptight boy, who was actually a man, wanting to shed, and finally experience the feeling of love.

I think back to when Obama won the election that November. There was cheering in the streets, and the windows of my railroad-style, just-moved-into Williamsburg apartment were kept open. The months that followed felt aimless. I was scared of loss after the first time a man held my hand while we slept, but I was not sleeping at all, too energized by his touch. I had no money and no job besides temporary writing gigs. My body felt constricted, made tighter by not having financial security, and not having yet experienced fully exploring with another man.

Maybe I was just a blank canvas, and not ready to accept or admit my naïveté. Now that I can, it's stuck there, in time, in memory, in me.

August 26

I'm flying to Florida on Sunday to stay with my mom for four days. It's been six years since I've been back home. I'm going for no other reason, really, than to see her and my father, because I don't know what the future holds. Maybe we, or I, keep looking to the past as a way to navigate going forward, because we don't know what the future is, if someone we love may die from Covid-19, or if a change in administration in January may alter how the virus is treated.

I'm accepting that death will inevitably come, and I'm accepting that I may not know when or for whom.

It would be quite tragic if I contracted Covid-19 on the airplane, and Death showed up on my mother's doorstep, and it was me. Trust me, she would give a dramatic hospital death-bed speech that may go something like this:

'Jay, you are my greatest gift, my contribution to the world. You are my art. And with my dying breath I... I... I...' [sound of heart monitor flatlining]

She would say it was worth it to see me.

I don't believe that it is Death itself that I fear or the physical decline of the body.

It is time that seems to have a will of its own, and it does not let anyone in on its intention or design.

August 27

Last night, I posted my own quote on Instagram:

'Time seems to have a will of its own and it does not let anyone in on its intention or design.'

Noah, the guy who I wondered if he was going to write again after he said he'd line my insides with cum, saw it and responded. He told me that he only believes in the illusion of free will but that free will does not actually exist. We shared our thoughts on time, and I said that time may be a plane, where the past, present, and future are all playing at once. I told him that somewhere in the future, he and I are hiking. He said he wanted to kiss me while he thought of a Pascal quote: *'I know neither my condition or duty, but to fuck you.'* He paraphrased that last part.

So, who is Noah, I ask. For one, he's a potential romantic: the second time we message each other, he references Pascal and we talk of time and space. The skeptical side of me asks, how many has he lured in with his words and romanticism? The other part of me feels a sense of luck that he could perhaps be a new person to know, and someone who I have the chance to explore with. The curious side of myself feels a sense of danger, because this does not feel like a friendship or a 'cum comradery.' I do not want too much of him, that I can say.

I think of Matthew, and I think of our calm, stable marriage that offers me endless affection. Isn't this what I wanted? To have everything, like time on a plane, playing out at once. To devote my time and love to my husband, to also have a lover, an exploratory lover who is heavy but whose weight I do not have to carry. To have a husband who I made vows to in front of loved ones, to be by his side until death, and a lover, whose time with me will be filled with fucking and philosophy.

Is this what I've wanted?

August 28

When I crave something, especially something new, it takes all of my attention, to the point that I want to chew it, eat it, swallow it, have it sit in me until it is broken down and digested.

It's always been like this.

I desire someone most when I have yet to have had the chance to have them. Maybe it's my imagination that I lust over.

More than once I've been told, 'You're a little intense.'

August 29

By the time I reached thirty, the men who I had dated earned a nickname for themselves: *The Lost Boys*. Without my grip, they would slip away into the night, and I wouldn't know if I would hear from them again. I don't think they knew what it was like to sleep by someone familiar. I chased them, and it is... or was... a quality of mine that could be described as a flaw. I remember thinking... if I didn't reach out for them, they'd fly away.

I don't want *them* to come back, someone who wanders in, looks around, takes what they need and moves on.

In the summer of 2014, I sat alone almost every night in my backyard, with a bottle of wine and a pack of cigarettes. I asked myself, why? Why does nothing stick with me? Why am I always chasing someone and then holding onto them to stay near?

What was it that attracted them? Was it my affinity for a bad romance? And what made them stop coming around and for Matthew to appear?

When I met Matthew that fall, I was unsure why this person wanted to curl into me as he did. I could say anything I wanted to him and he'd always laugh a little, always listening. At the time, I had been working evening shifts at a historic hotel, outside of Times Square. I worked the night of Thanksgiving, and when my days off came, Matthew invited me to his apartment. There, he prepped and cooked a three-course meal, including a turkey and pumpkin pie, so we could celebrate Thanksgiving together. We had known each other for only three weeks.

August 30

I'm waiting to board a flight at LGA to Fort Lauderdale. The airport, thankfully, is not crowded. I was nervous this morning when getting ready to fly. I guess the thought of flying during a pandemic isn't a relaxing one. It's been six years since I've been back to Florida, and I like that this trip feels quiet. I didn't tell one friend who lives there that I was coming down.

I want to be in a different location, at least for a bit.

Maybe it can relieve certain anxieties I've been having. I was thinking of Noah, and thought, what intimacy does he want with me that he cannot get from anyone else? Am I just a body? A sensual feeling and a body?

I thought of Leo, who asked me to visit him in New Paltz in September. I thought about the stupid memes he sends on a daily basis and the awkward, even embarrassing moments we've had during sex. Despite those moments, or maybe because of them, he's asked me to come back and see him again. I think of Matthew, this morning, after I woke up early and paced a bit, then crawled back into bed. He touched my hand and said, 'I'm glad you're back.'

My thoughts round back to Noah.

> *'I want to line your insides with my cum, to fuck naked in the woods, to put my fingers in your mouth, for you to hop on my dick as I kiss you gently,' he wrote.*

I mean, isn't fucking bareback in the woods what every gay man wants to experience? Isn't that the equivalent to a straight woman bursting into tears when her boyfriend finally gets on one knee and pops the question? It's what everyone wants.

I realized then that someone who quotes Blaise Pascal, as Noah did, and says they want to cum inside you, is someone that you won't ever hear from again.

August 31, 6:53 am

It's Monday morning, around 7 am, and I slept soundly in my mother's bed (she slept on the couch at her own insistence). This bed feels like you could fall into it, and the bedroom turns pitch black when the blinds are drawn. I don't think I woke up even once. Carrie (my mom) and I spent the majority of the afternoon and evening going through a giant bin filled with family pictures dating back to the nineties, eighties, seventies, and some even from the 1940s. It was part an organizational effort on her behalf (she is always organizing), and part going down memory lane. It wasn't really a stroll down memory lane as much as it was a 'What the fuck?' and 'Do you remember that?' So much was documented in the past, and I thought about how disposable cameras would encourage you to use up a roll of film just so you could get it developed as quickly as possible.

Tomorrow, I'm doing the same thing when I visit my dad: going through piles of pictures. This isn't really an organizational effort on his behalf as much as it's him doling out photographs between his kids. I'm guessing I'll be receiving the oldest ones, and I hope there are some of his side of the family while they lived in Jamaica, when life did not resemble what it was to become.

I'm mentioning all of this because I am at a stage of collecting *what was*.

Something has broken or ended within myself, and possibly within my family, too. The dramatic narrative of my parents fighting, my two older half-siblings being split between homes, me being a withdrawn, moody outcast is coming to a close. That narrative of brokenness, of constantly being torn between people, does not hold the same relevance that it once did. The content became stale over the years. It was once an effective storyline, best suited for an eighties and nineties audience: a primetime TV family drama that lasted for a few too many seasons after it reached its peak. And now, it is going off the air.

So, I am collecting what was. This trip, in a way, feels like an epilogue, and I'm okay with that. It took a long time to get through the chapters that led here.

9:44 pm

I wrote this morning that a toxic family narrative was gone, and then this happened today: I fought with my mother, who made an announcement on Facebook that I was in Florida when I asked her not to. I thought no one knew I was visiting and then a slew of text messages came in, friends asking when I came down followed by at least four question marks.

As I walked into her living room, I asked, 'Mom, did you post anything on Facebook about me being here?'

She paused, with a frown on her face, as if recalling if she did such a thing.

'I, uh, I did, Jay.'

'Okay, I... I didn't want anyone knowing I was here, because it's awkward, and I wanted to quarantine without having to deal with that.'

'Well, I didn't know you were still feeling that way. I just didn't know,' she said.

'Alright, bu—'

That last opposition, that 'but' I said is what opened Pandora's box. She told me that I made her feel as if she's not allowed to be proud of her son. That she's doing everything wrong as a mother. That she walks on eggshells around me. We fought to a point that I was looking up flights to leave this evening. To the point that I aimed my finger at her and venomously said, 'You've been doing this since I was five years old.'

I, along with her, am able to identify what triggers our fights. Sometimes, I feel like she will say or do something that will make the ground fall from underneath me. She then senses my distance. This feeling, of me being far from her, makes her feel abandoned. And despite all of this knowledge, despite all of the red flags along the way to stop while we're ahead, these fights still happen.

I'm angry at her and at the fact that I have taken on some of her behaviors that I complain about. I am angry at her dramatizations, her accusations, her claiming that I abandon her. What upsets me, truly upsets me, is when our voices escalate and she says 'I won't take your abuse.' I hear that word, 'abuse,' and I come undone. I've heard it so many times, too many times. I want her to see that when I confront her about something, she takes this criticism so harshly, so hard to heart, that she interprets it as me calling her a failure. That's when she takes that hurt and hurls it back at me. Then she walks away.

She comes back when she is ready, puts on a sweet, almost child-like voice, and acts like nothing happened. She's done this before, and I try to be mindful and calm, but this is when I *pop*. It's when I own up to losing my shit, not so much my temper, but more so... my mind. I pop because I cannot just ride the fucking rollercoaster that we're on. I wonder if that's why I choose to write. I need my version of how I think and feel to be seen by another because for thirty years I've been an unwilling rider on Space Mountain or Tower of Terror, or whatever ride it is that we're battling to control.

I want to believe what I wrote this morning, but there is obviously something larger at play. I don't know what it is, if it's just simple family patterns, dynamics, and psychology. What I thought was a closing of a book, an ending of bad habits and communication, now feels like a grainy black and white movie playing on a loop.

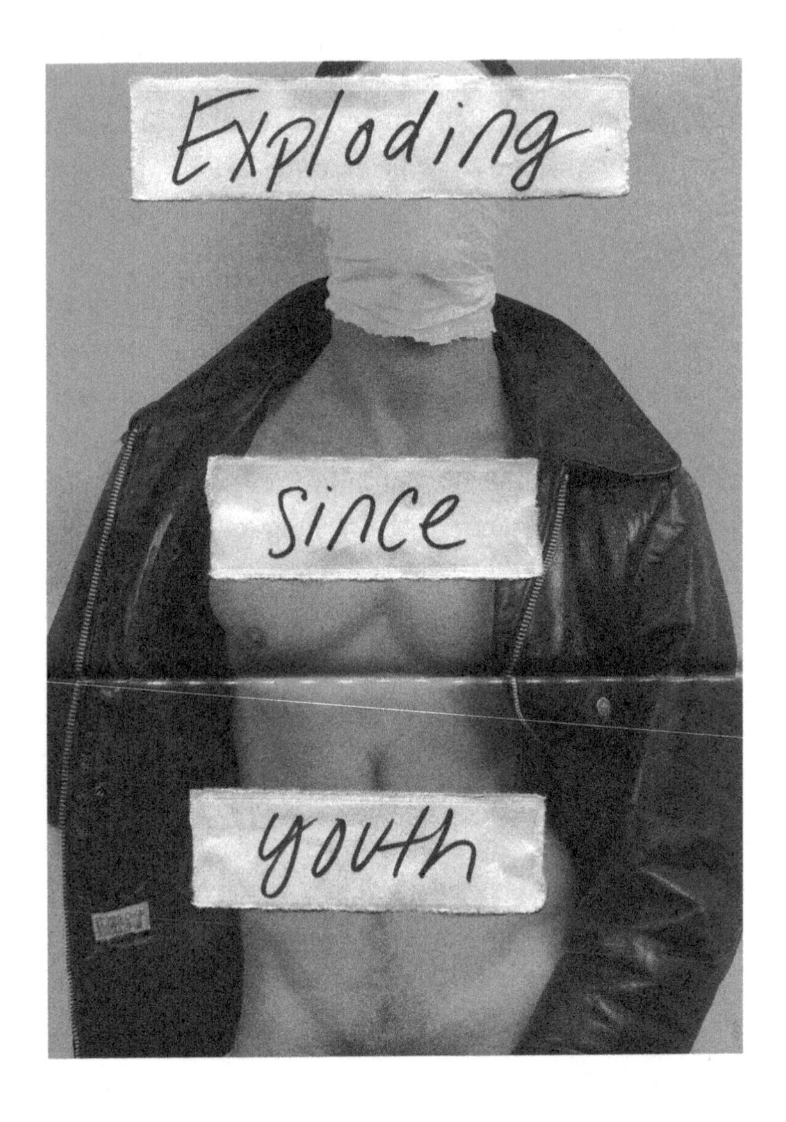
Exploding
since
youth

SEPTEMBER 2020

September 1

My dad gave me piles of photographs of his side of the family; some of the pictures dated back to the late 1800s. I want to look at them, study them, find stories for them, and try to understand them.

When I got back to my mom's, she sat with me looking over the photographs for about an hour, with an interest almost as strong as my own. We couldn't turn back our fight from last night, but as always, we agreed to move on. With photographs scattered all over the kitchen counter, she then got up from her chair with a look of concern on her face.

She said, 'I've received some news today.'

'Okay...'

'I had some medical tests come back, and it looks like I have cancer cells.'

I told her I was sorry. I hugged her, and she began to cry, but did not break down. She's going to get further testing. I told her if she needs an operation that I would fly down and help her recover.

September 3

Sitting alone at a beach in Fort Lauderdale, the air is warm with a strong breeze. The sound of the ocean is continuous, soft and loud. I'm grateful for this moment of solitude, smells of sea salt, and the tanning of my skin. Maybe I'm a little sad thinking of how I didn't visit here for six years. Something seems naïve about it, like I thought I was changing or altering something by being away. In reality, I've always been here, just not physically.

September 5

I don't have a plan for the future. I have about seven grand in the bank and no job prospects since I've been furloughed. I've thought about spending my savings and starting a printing press, or maybe I'll get my Masters in Library Sciences. Or maybe I won't. There are some days, like today, when I feel as if I'm free-floating. I wonder, what time or place is this feeling comparable to? It must have been when I was 23, just graduated college, with no plan.

The question that I asked then and I ask now is: Do I even want a plan?

I mean, what were my immediate options as a 23-year-old closeted college grad with a Creative Writing degree? To get a quaint one-bedroom apartment in Pompano Beach, and write for the *Sun-Sentinel* newspaper, and live what appeared to be a quiet life of an asexual while my mother tells me that a psychic told her that she was going to have two grandbabies one day? Is that what I was going to do? Well, fourteen years later, with no job and the possible death of the hospitality industry... this predicament has opened a forum for others to express their questions, concerns and suggestions regarding my future.

'You're going to be forty soon, and I want to see you doing what you really love.'

'You should get a dog. I can see you as a dog-dad.'

'You and Matthew should buy a car.'

'You and Matthew should move upstate.'

'Do you think you'll have kids?'

'I think you're ready for a plant.'

Maybe I want to sit home, and write, and trim my backyard once a week, and watch Turner Classic Movies, and be silly with my husband in the mornings, and complain about others and their Instagrams, and not get a dog, and not think about children, and I'll collect unemployment and not make any moves right now.

Back then, thirteen or fourteen years ago, in Florida, I didn't make any decisive, definitive moves. Instead, I waited.

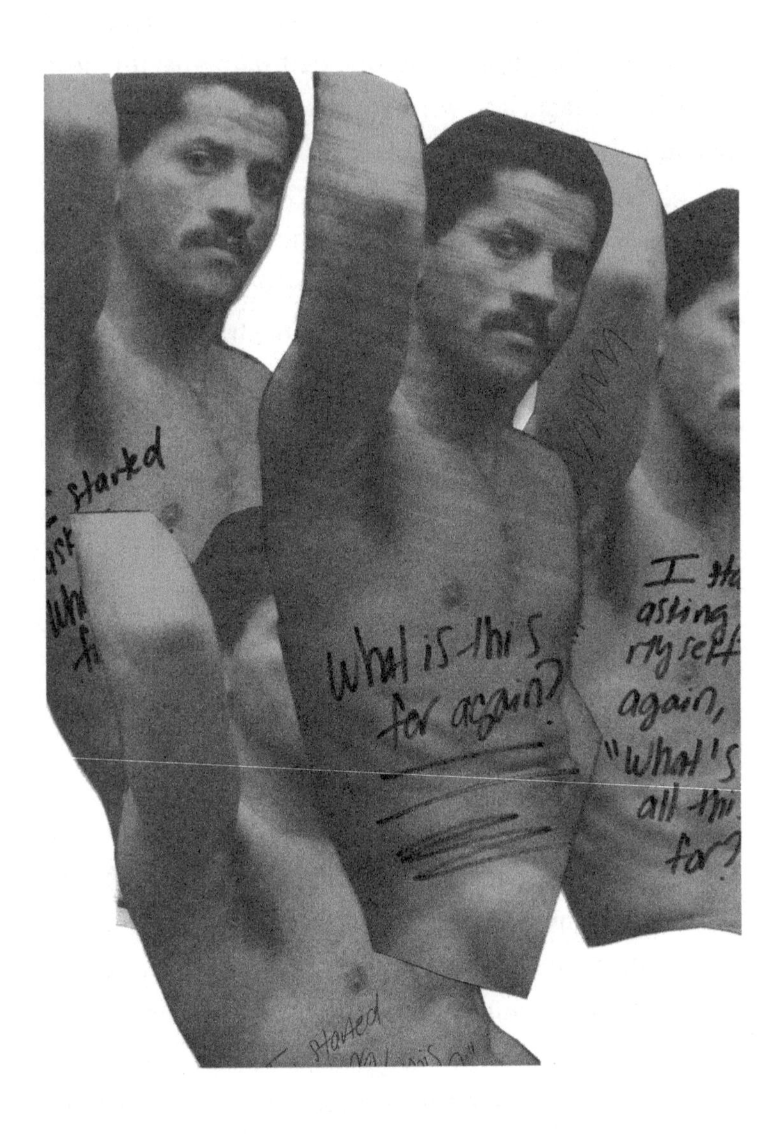
started
What is this
for again?
asking
myself
again,
"What's
for?

September 6

The first time I invited someone over for sex, without Matthew there, was the day after Christmas of last year. Matthew was out of town visiting his family in Oregon, and I had just worked back-to-back shifts over Christmas at the hotel. I didn't plan that morning, the morning of the 26th, to invite anyone over. I woke up very hungover (when I would drink throughout the night and wake up after a couple hours of sleep, that is when my horniness was at its peak). It was like I needed to fuck the whiskey out of my system.

I found someone online; he was in his late-thirties, went by the name 'latinbi3,' and couldn't host because he had a wife and kids at home. He drove nearly thirty miles to me from Long Island to Brooklyn and arrived around 1:30 pm. I had only seen a picture of his cock, not his face nor his body, as he described himself as *discreet*. Besides, I didn't care what he looked like. There was an element, perhaps a large element, the element of secrecy that turned me on. It felt like true cruising. There was not a polite getting-to-know-you conversation beforehand. If both parties are only looking for a transactional intimacy, do we really need to know where one grew up, what they do for a living, or how they like to spend their spare time?

When he showed up at my doorstep, he wore large, reflective, silver sunglasses. I can't remember if he ever took them off. He was a large man, at least 230 pounds, maybe more, broad shouldered, clean shaven, with a bulging belly showing through his weekday business attire. He stood in my living room and immediately began to undress. He was breathing heavily when his pants hit the floor. I undressed too, and we stood naked in front of one another. We did not kiss. Instead, he grabbed my flesh like he wanted to caress it but wasn't sure how. He sat down on the couch, opened his legs, and I bent down and started to suck him. His cock was fleshy, smaller than Matthew's, although most are. The faster I went, the deeper he breathed. He seemed like he didn't have much time, so I stood up and led him to the bedroom.

'Lay on your back,' I said.

He laid on my bed, sprawled across the duvet. I handed him a condom, which he hurriedly put on. Stretching my legs across his waist, I eased him into me, and began to move back and forth, side to side. Maybe his glasses were off at this point, because I remember his face having a look of disbelief (I could be imagining this in my recollection). As I rode him, the slats on the underside of my bed that supported the mattress gave out. The bed partially collapsed, startling him. I motioned for him to pay it no mind.

Suddenly, he flipped me onto my back, put my legs around his shoulders, and started fucking me. He was moving fast and deep, but the feeling was tolerable since his dick was of average size. I looked at his hands; we were both wearing our wedding rings. He pulled himself out of me, threw the condom on the side of the bed, and jerked off onto my stomach. I'm pretty sure we came at the same time. He couldn't have spoken more than three words as we dressed. After he left, a lingering scent of cheap cologne filled the apartment. I didn't mind.

Matthew came home later that night, or it may have been the night after. I told him that I invited someone over and we fucked. I had been nervous the whole day, knowing that I was going to say something. When I started speaking, the words just came out easily. I described the guy, telling Matthew he was married and to a woman. Matthew sat there, listening, with a smile on his face and a curious gleam of curiosity in his eye.

September 7

I avoided dating via hook-up apps forever. The first one I signed up for was OKCupid in the winter of 2013. I wasn't even on them for that long since I met Matthew, via Scruff, in October of the next year. From there, we bathed in monogamy for two years. So, as I descend into my memory bank, I ask myself, how did I meet other gay men if not through the internet? I'll say this first: I thought I was better than the apps. Some egotistical part of me felt above them, like they were for desperate, dick-hungry men who needed to speed-up time to get cock. I mean, that still rings true, but the difference is that now I think there's nothing wrong or shameful about it. My judgment was strong because my denial of how much I wanted sex was stronger. Also, I wanted someone who was intensely attracted to me, more than just physically; I wanted to live in their brain. Having my picture in a little square box with a green light next to it, in a selection pool of thousands, wasn't enough. So, I resisted.

This left me with limited options, especially since I didn't frequent gay bars, much less with the intention of picking someone up. So... who did I date and how did I meet them? There was Dan, who I had been introduced to at a Thanksgiving dinner in Brooklyn. Dan was weird, attractive, eccentric, quiet, and I couldn't tell if he was ever being serious or not. There was Domorique, a ninteen-year-old model for Tommy Hilfiger and *Vibe* magazine. He was a child with nowhere to go, and I've been known to collect strays. Anyways, he was introduced to me through a co-worker and mutual friend. There was Reggie, who changed identities and looks every six months. Reggie was the first to hold my hand while we, or he, slept. His best friend was my first roommate in New York. And then... there was C.K., my first same-sex kiss, sexual experience, and boyfriend. C.K. should have his own page dedicated to him but recalling my time with him proves to be more confusing than revealing. The first time I saw him, he was dressed in all black and snakily walking up stairs at a nightclub. We passed each other, and he looked at me like he was going to either fuck me or kill me. He succeeded at the former, the latter I'm still partially convinced he might have tried at some point.

And there was Victor, who I picked-up late night at a bodega, and who I was determined to keep.

I had a habit, back in 2012, of buying 40s late at night with a handful of loosie-cigarettes. It felt ritualistic, especially since I told myself each time that I was only going to buy one 40 and two loosies. Then 30–40 minutes later, I'd be back at the bodega to buy more. It created a sense of control, even if it was a false one. One night at the bodega on the corner of 181st and Broadway, there was a handsome Dominican man at the counter, talking the ear off of the cashier. They may have known each other, or they may have been total strangers. Sometimes, it's hard to tell. He was suave-looking, had small black-brown eyes, wavy jet-black hair, and a smile that I could tell he used very often. When I placed my 40 on the counter, he turned to me and said, 'Nice glasses.'

He was reading my reaction. 'Thanks,' I said coolly.

What he didn't know or remember was that almost a year earlier, we sat next to each other on the train, in silence, both reading our books. Minutes earlier, he had spotted me on the subway platform and walked about thirty feet toward me.

'Do you know if this train goes to Lincoln Center?' he asked.

He knew the answer to his own question. Judging from his walk, he was not a tourist.

'Yea, just take this to 66th,' I said.

We didn't say anything else, only stood there. I didn't know what else to say and for me, his presence was enough.

At the bodega, under his inquisitive looks, I again was silent. Grabbing my 40, I pushed open the door making the little bell attached to it to ring, and walked out. I crossed to 181st and was back on my block between Broadway and Fort Washington. *I should have fucking said something*, I thought. Just go back. He's probably still there, just go back. I turned around, crossing Broadway, hoping he'd still be there. And there he was, standing out front, smoking a cigarette.

'I wanted to say hi before, but didn't. I'm Jason.'

'I'm Victor,' he said.

Victor was the first person I said 'I love you' to. He lived in my tiny room for three weeks out of the six months we were together. I tried to break-up with him once, but he wouldn't let me. It was always difficult to stay in touch with Victor, to retain a closeness with him. Yet, when I tried to finally pull away, he sat on the edge of my bed in his wrinkled white T-shirt, with tears in his eyes. When I said I wanted to break-up, he only said, 'I can't let you go'. That was in the beginning of fall and by New Year's Eve, when he left me alone waiting for him, I knew then it was time to say goodbye.

Years later, I saw Victor in a bar, around 2 am, in Hell's Kitchen. I knew it was him, even though I could only see the back of his dyed bleach-blond hair. I knew it was him by the way his shoulders moved and how he leaned into the young man who faced him. Downing at least three shots, my courage grew and I yelled 'Victor,' my voice cutting across the loud music. He turned and saw me, immediately smiled, his face plastered with a look of surprise. Leaping off his bar stool to come say hello, the young man he was with stared straight ahead, appearing unbothered.

September 8

Everyone is entitled to their own version of queerness, whatever it may be. Often it's a fantasy; a flowery oasis, a utopia, a unicorn, a reconciliation of pain.

For me? I can't do much with flowers and rainbows, but I can go inside the color black.

Where is the harshness?
Where is the hardness?
Where is the rock-n-roll?
Where is the angry Queer?
Where is the angsty Queer?
Where is the Queer individual?
Where is the individual?

September 9

The need to connect with other Queers does not go away. It is essential and human to want to find others like yourself. That, I feel, we all have in common. Then where do we go from there? The fact that I desire connection through touch (and sometimes combine sex with friendship), while other Queers preach that physicality can ruin Queer friendships... that creates a rift in me.

And it is not the suggestion of platonic love that bothers me, there are many kinds of love, but rather, it is the sermon-like way on social media that it is delivered: 'NORMALIZE PLATONIC QUEER LOVE! THE MOST HONEST LOVE OF ALL.' I have a difficult time reading or hearing Queers preach to other Queers about what's best for each other: especially when it comes from the same persons who have likely felt a lack of ownership or authority over their own lives at some point.

And I do get it: as Queer people, particularly gay men, it's imbedded on some level that we are the most viable, and the most wanted if we are sexual and participating in sex and are desired by others. I understand that the response to that, even a rebellion from that mindset is to showcase how lovely Queer friendship is and how it can resemble a family. I don't want to take that away from anyone, that's not my intent. It is easily understood that community keeps its members alive and in more ways than one. Maybe I should share that I never sought out a platonic Queer family in the sense that friends resembled nuclear family members. It never occured to me to do so since I did not seek to be enveloped in someone's care, whole-heartedly, who could not be my lover.

Because I often walk in solitude, I too have felt like I haven't belonged, even when I'm around Queer people who are considered my peers. Sometimes in a crowd of gay cis men, I feel like I'm Gomez Addams walking into the slumber party in *Grease* as they're singing 'Sandra

Dee'. I'm not even the outcast Sandy in that scenario whose feelings are at first hurt but who finds a way to blend and eventually be a part of the Pink Ladies. Instead, I am Gomez, wearing a thin mustache and a look of bewilderment, not understanding the pressure to be uniform with his surroundings. So, when I see memes and infographics posted over and over again on Instagram, by Queers, declaring what the truest form of Queer love is, I wonder, Who is this declaration for? Why am I being told this? And I ask myself, why do I care like I do?

September 10

Normally, I would not write about Manhattan because I am not one of those New Yorkers who idolizes the city. I, like many, many other Queers in their twenties, moved to New York to find myself, to feel creative or free, or whatever that age-old story is. After twelve years, I've grown indifferent to the city. I acknowledge that New York is this center, or like a fortune cookie, that is able to tell what is about to happen elsewhere in the country. There is, still, a certain sense of pride in living in a place where *things* happen first. Yet, for the life of me, I cannot understand when New Yorkers say they 'miss riding the subway' since the pandemic caused the city to shut down. I'm sorry, but get fucking real, do you actually miss being on top of sweaty strangers at rush hour, breathing on you, the air filling with tension? If that rings true for you, you are just as much a tourist as you are a New Yorker.

I've only been back in Manhattan a handful of times since March. Two of the three times, it was to get to Amtrak at Penn Station when I visited Leo upstate. The third time was for the Queer Liberation for Black Lives rally. Even then, I was marching, while masked, in a crowd of 50,000 people. I wasn't exactly taking in Manhattan and surveying my surroundings, maybe except for the cops that lined the perimeters of the march, one of whom made sure we saw how tightly he clutched his club.

Yesterday, I went back for a fourth time to drop off a writing anthology (I edited earlier this summer) to an art gallery/gift shop about to launch a 'socially-distanced' (re)opening. The Union Square station, in midafternoon, was at best a third full of what it normally had been. The majority of people wore masks, and there was room to walk, even do a spin or a twirl if you wanted to. There was no rush, no one bumping into you in order to make their appointment or punch into work on time. It was not dead, but it moved slower than usual, like someone walking after an injury.

Fifth, 6th and 7th Ave. were completely devoid of travelers and tourists. Local businesses were open, many of the owners stood outside, masked, arms crossed, surveying the streets. There were local peddlers and drug dealers who have always been there but were once shrouded by crowds. Now, they are the main attraction, even if some of their business is lost. I turned the corner onto 8th Ave. and looked up at Homecoming, my now closed-down hotel. My last day of work, before being furloughed, was on March 15th. All of the windows were boarded with panels of wood, spray-painted black. They were painted black in order to blend; to camoflauge. I guess a wooden board in its natural state suggests loss, lack of income, cheapness, or neglect. A black board, though, looks like Death. It looked like Death stopped by and was not yet ready to leave.

I walked to the center of the street to snap a picture of the front of the building.

'Jason!' someone called.

I looked over and saw Lobsang, one of the hotel's housemen, wearing a T-shirt with the hotel's logo, standing along the side of the building.

'Hey!'

I may have yelled my hello, as I was not expecting to see anyone I used to work with. To be honest, I didn't think he would be working at all.

'What are you doing here?' I asked.

'I'm working,' he said.

'Oh, I didn't even... wait, doing what?'

'Ah, you know, taking care of the building, the grounds...'

'Oh, okay. Do you know anything about the reopening?' I asked.

I realized the humor in asking this: me, his one-time manager, asking him about the reopening. But he is a Union employee and let's face it, the Union is who really runs things.

His eyes squinted, looking a little perplexed. 'Ah, you know. They keep giving dates, then pushing back. Giving dates, then pushing back. Maybe we'll reopen in October,' he said.

'Yea, maybe, you know... well, I'm really glad I got to see you. It's been crazy, hasn't it?'

'In April, no one here. No one. It was like a ghost town. Now, it's coming back to life a little,' he said.

'Yea, well, hopefully...'

We said our goodbyes, and I walked down the sidewalk and felt happy. Happy to see someone I used to see on a daily basis. He and I were working together the night the pipes busted in the walls and gushing hot water caused the ceilings to cave in on five floors. Lobsang stood there, knee-deep in water, plaster floating around him. We were yelling over the sound of rushing water, asking each other what we needed.

September 11

'Do you want a flag?' someone yelled out to me.

I just entered the entrance to Greenwood Cemetery, and the man at the security gate (who I've never heard talk) was speaking to me.

'Do you want a flag?' he repeated.

Something didn't register with me. What does he mean?

'Do you want a flag? For September 11th?'

I saw that he was holding a cheap dollar store American flag in his hand.

'Oh, uh, no... no, I don't need one.'

It's a gloomy-ish, quiet day in New York, overcast with a constant breeze. This morning, I kept the television on a low volume as the 3,000 names of persons lost on 9/11 were read. On the corner of the screen were pictures of the dead, their names and their ages. I took a mental note every time I saw someone around the age of 37 or 38. I thought, enough years have passed that these people and their images are now from another era. The pictures shown in the corner of the screen were probably all taken in the nineties or even the year 2000. It's like the ones who've died are cemented in that time, while the rest of us move on.

Maybe we're cemented in time right now, too. Stuck, in a pandemic, not moving, touching, creating with one another as we once did. The only thing we can do right now is wait. Hopefully, I can build something during this time; something that becomes stuck in amber.

September 12

For the most part, when someone asks me, 'how are you doing' (during the pandemic), I give the same answer.

'Ultimately, I'm grateful to have had this time off. I've been creating so much more. Matthew is good. He and I both do our own thing while we're home...'

Being sequestered like this for six months, with all of this quiet and so much inaction, is starting to set off tiny bombs in me. I'm not sure when they are about to detonate and neither does Matthew, which for us, makes matters worse.

A few minutes ago, around 9:30 am, we were sitting in our living room. The TV is off (it's usually on at that time) and I am on my phone reading a story about how Trump influenced the CDC to lie about Covid stats and facts. To the left, at my ankle, is Sid, a terrier type of dog that we're taking care of for the weekend while her owner, a friend of mine, is out of town. She hears a faint sound, although to her it might be thunderous, in the hallway of our apartment building. She begins to bark. She has a high-pitched bark that sounds like little screams.

'Sid,' Matthew says.

He says her name in an effort to tell her she should not be barking. There's hardly any authority in his voice.

'Sid,' he lethargically repeats.

Still, she barks. Tiny, chirping screams. She pays no attention to him.

And she barks some more.

'Sid,' he says again.

There is the slightest tone of irritation in his voice, but nothing that would cause an animal to cease what it is doing.

She continues to bark.

Without any preconceived notion of what I was about to do, I grabbed a butter knife sitting in front of me. I picked the knife up and plunged it straight into the table. It enters the soft, cheap wood as if it is cheese. I slam the knife on the table, causing a loud metallic clang. Matthew jerks backwards, startled. He blinks quickly, his eyelids shutter. Sid, the dog, runs to Matthew and sits next to him. Now, she is silent.

A lack of force, indecision, or air thick with apathy stirs something in me. It makes me feel alone, like I'm wandering on a planet with no likeness of life or existence near me. It's as though my frustration must cut through the air of nothingness in order to create... something... anything.

After I got a little 'knife happy' as Mrs Loomis in *Scream 2* would say, I laid in bed for 45 minutes. I needed all of the questions swirling in my head to come to rest.

What am I doing here?
Am I happy?
Am I impossible?
Do I have what I need?
If I don't, is that anyone's fault?
I've never lived alone.
I never learned how to cook.
I never decorated a home like it was mine.
Did I fuck up my past?
Is my future dead?

I knew I could not stay in my room forever, and I knew that Matthew was patiently sitting on the couch. I walked into the living room, where he was, waiting. Sid saw me, jumped down, wagging her tail, and barked, or screamed or loudly chirped. Her nails were making clickety-clack sounds on the wooden floor. I sat next to Matthew.

'I'm sorry,' I said.

He wrapped his arms around me, resting his chin between my neck and shoulder.

'I love you,' he said.

'I love you.'

September 13

Years ago, in Miami, a friend and I were snorting uppers off the middle console in my car, before we went to see the band Ladytron play a show. I have or had, always enjoyed an upper. I mean, I still do, except now it's caffeine and lots of it. Anyway, feeling high and high on ourselves, we walked a haughty walk, skipping a line of concert-goers wrapped around the building. My friend and I did not need to wait in a line, and we let it show. Head after head turned to look at us, perhaps wondering why *we* did not have to wait like *them*.

How long does a high like that last? That feeling that you're controlling the environment around you. It only lasts a moment and that moment is never enough.

Whatever I want to present or wish to present to others, something unexpected usually flies in and fucks it up. Even now, as you read this, I ask myself, is there a point in editing it so that it may fit the intent of what it is I'd like you to see? No, because you're going to read something between the lines that I am blind to and cannot control.

Sex, in many ways, is anti-control. I do not know what the other person may do, or how my body will react. Me and another could talk about fucking all we want, but the tumbling, the submission, the smell, and the mechanics take on an unpredictable life of their own. And in a time and place and world where it seems control has no use for me, I look to what seems to be one of the only things that matters: when someone wants to spend their time with you.

Sometimes, I don't know why Matthew wants to be around me or why he tells me he loves me as much as he does. I am moody, shifty, depressed at times, and more anxious than what is considered 'normal.' Still, he seems happy to be with me. I don't have to ask myself why I am with him. He can alter a scene, a situation, or scenario and make it light or child-like. His point-of-view affects mine, as I am continuously surprised that he is able to see the world painted in such bright colors.

September 14

It's now 6:08 am, and I've been up for over 45 minutes. I felt energized when I got up, and the bedroom was so cold from the A/C being on all night. The outside temperature has dropped, and it no longer feels like summer. The weekend of the 25th, I've made plans to go back to New Paltz and visit Leo. I'm planning on meeting an old friend and co-worker in Nyack first, and Leo may meet me and drive me up from there. I heard a hot air balloon competition or show or something will take place in Nyack over the weekend. I guess you're supposed to watch it from the confines of your car, which in my opinion, makes it all the better.

I thought of how it was Leo who suggested that I come see him again. I missed him this morning, the feeling of his compact, hairy body in bed. I thought of his, I guess you could say, complex relationship with intimacy. He fucks when he's hungry for it and there is violence in his thrusts. Often, when Leo felt horny, he'd play a hardcore video on his TV, and he and I would jerk off together. He's well-stocked on lube, and he doesn't let time rush him. Sitting side-by-side, watching two men 69 on screen, I once suggested that we fuck missionary with him on top. He told me, bluntly, that he had hesitation to do so. To him, this suggested a heightened intimacy because of the close proximity of our eyes and faces. I listened while he spoke, and it was, to me, a bold thing for him to admit his hesitance. I also told him a truth: I wanted to have more control during our sex. He didn't respond much as I told him this, but nodded his head to show that he was listening.

Later that night, when we both were nude, I climbed on top of him, carefully. He moaned when he felt himself slip inside.

'You're so warm,' he told me.

I moved my hips, with minimal motion at first. As I gained momentum, he thrust himself hard, sending a burst of pressure inside me. He could have just been overly excited, or he could have been demonstrating his dominance or control.

'Easy,' I said.

He had a smirk on his face and placed his hands behind his head. This is most certainly my favorite position to find a man in: on his back, with his arms up. It is a showcase of one's masculinity, of the hair on their body, of the muscles underneath their skin.

I started to moan, not only for him, but for the pressure he was putting inside me.

'Jason, this is so hot.'

I knew that it was, and I was aware of how much hotter it would be if I came while he was still inside me. I quickened my pace.

'I'm going to cum really soon,' I said.

Leo's body moved up and down in a vertical motion on the bed, his arms making an A-shape above his head.

'Fuck, I'm cumming.'

Cum shot out of me, landing on Leo's fur-lined stomach and sternum. I climbed off of him, looking at his penis, still hard, shiny, and lubed. I expected him to start jerking off, to finish. Instead, he got up, walked to the bathroom and washed himself off. As he re-emerged, he smiled. There was a proud glow to him, a sereneness. He kissed me on the mouth, with a look of satisfaction on his face.

When I thought of Leo this morning, I thought it would be nice for him to know that I missed him. It could be good for him to know that someone misses him.

September 15

Late last year, I signed up on Squirt.org, a site specializing in cruising and public sex. Now, I really just use it for voyeur purposes, especially during these pandemic times. I chose to not sign up for Grindr. I wanted something smaller, or less... like Grindr. Grind'r always reminded me of real-estate. People are paraded like new homes, and the buyers prefer the plainest model. There are elements of conformity and commercialism in the whole thing that I found boring and off-putting.

When I was active on Squirt, someone (we'll call him Anon) messaged me, with no profile picture or information about himself, and offered to jerk off with me in a bathroom in a nearby Target. The proposition, which I've never had before, left me feeling nervous but more than nervous, I was curious. I got on the R train, walked briskly to Target which was located at a very busy intersection in a shopping mall in downtown Brooklyn. Once there, I received a message with directions of where to go. Anon said that he would be in jeans and a black shirt and that he'd be inside the bathroom, waiting for me. After circling the aisles of Target, trying and probably failing to look inconspicuous, I found the restrooms. My heart was beating on the outside of my chest. I opened the restroom door. I didn't see anyone inside.

I stepped in and to my right saw a stall with the door slightly ajar. Anon was standing inside. He looked young, mid-twenties, clean-cut, had dark hair that looked like it had drugstore gel in it. He had a thin frame, wore semi-baggy blue jeans, had tan skin and big, dark brown eyes. He smiled a little at me, and motioned his head to the left, signalling that we should go into the stall next door. I opened the door to the accessible stall, and he followed me inside.

Immediately, he began unbuckling his pants, and I did the same. I wasn't hard yet; I was too nervous to be hard. He slipped his jeans and briefs underwear down to his ankles. His pubes looked like they were in the process of growing back in after being shaven, a typical aesthetic for straight men, that to me looked like the year 2000. On his left hand, he wore a chunky gold wedding band.

I lowered my pants to my knees, and we both began jerking. I started to get hard, and quick.

'Nice,' he said.

He was laser-focused on my dick, which was getting wet.

'We can't take long,' he whispered.

The door to the entrance of the bathroom swung open. Instinctively, I stood on my toes. I aligned my feet against the edges of the stall in such a way that they *might* be hidden from anyone trying to look in.

Anon, now my partner-in-crime, took his index finger and held it over his mouth. He stepped over to the toilet, his feet in plain view, probably with the purpose to look like he was peeing.

He kept jerking.

Holding myself tightly, without moving my hand, cum rose up and seeped through my fingertips. I took my hand, put it in my mouth, eating as much cum as I could so it wouldn't fall and make a splat sound on the tile floor.

Anon kept jerking. Holding his head and neck back, cum shot out of him, landing in the toilet water below. The entry door opened again, our intruder now gone.

Quickly, myself and Anon, my intimate stranger, pulled our pants up and buckled our belts. We opened the stall door and acted as if we'd never met. I performatively glanced at myself in the stained bathroom mirror. When we walked out of the bathroom, we separated and left going in different directions.

On the way to the train, and on the way home, I wondered if it was worth it, if the adrenalin overpowered the pleasure. Maybe that was the risk and the point of it all.

September 16

Mary MacLane wrote that her Portrayal meant everything to her, as if it was a marker of her existence, an announcement that said to others: I am living in this world, and you will be intrigued by me. If she didn't write her Portrayal, she could have been invisible.

I could rant and rave about how I cannot relate to 25-year-olds on Instagram, who have minimalist-styled apartments full of plants, bodies with lean muscle and no fat, and a solid career trajectory. I could ask, is this where we are as Queers, in particular Queer men? Is one's goal to resemble one of the affable, handsome, nature-loving Queers from *Queer Eye*; to market the hell out of a product and of themselves? *And now a word from our sponsors...*

Writing too much about the status-quo can be dull, but I'm reminded of what Mary could have felt: invisible for not meeting a norm. An exhausting thought is that now, in 2020, what goes against the norm has turned into opportunity for profit. If you are femme, fat, trans, there is likely a company or corporation biting at the bit to profit from your image, waiting to plaster your face and body on a billboard. Of course I believe in inclusion, representation, and equality and hope to be remembered as someone who lives by it and fights for it. Still I ask fellow Queers, is the end goal or symbol of success to find one's face on a billboard in a neutered Times Square? And if you are one who makes it on a poster that sits sky-high, have you questioned why you are there? Are you the face of inclusivity for a corporation or business trying to wiggle out of a PR pickle?

Mary MacLane didn't give a fuck and neither do I. I spent years waiting for another, hoping someone would make me or discover me or something of the sort. I don't think it works like that anymore. Maybe it's all a part of the Hollywood Dream, a result of the American Dream mentality that is embedded in Americans; so-and-so is going to come along and see me, discover me, make me and put me on a red carpet, the place I'm supposed to be.

Who knows, maybe I am where I am supposed to be right now, this second. On a bench in a cemetery at 10 am, stewing, contemplating where I'm meant to be. Perhaps I'm meant to stew. It's better than posing nude with a fucking houseplant hiding my dick, like everyone else, anxiously waiting for 'Likes' to pour in.

September 17

I try to not let certain intuitions dictate my reality. It is and has always been easy to fall inside of myself, to be obsessive with a feeling instead of a fact.

Today is my mom's birthday. She's turning 64. I wrote down on my calendar that she has a doctor's appointment on the 22nd. She's having her biopsy done then. We don't know anything yet, but I have a feeling the result may not be benign. Still, it's only a feeling. Her body and her health are a bit like her: unpredictable, wild, oddly resilient, but not always safe.

She was diagnosed with Type 1 diabetes when I was three years old. She was only thirty. As the story goes, we were in her car driving through South Carolina where we were visiting her parents and brother. What should have only been a half-hour car ride turned into three hours. Her blood sugar had dropped so low, and her thoughts became so clouded, that she could hardly find her way home. When we arrived at her parents house, her mother (who is also diabetic) pricked my mom's finger and tested her blood sugar.

'Not my daughter!' her mother said.

Supposedly, she slammed her fist on the kitchen table as she yelled this. It seemed like a pretty strong, dramatic reaction to have, but it is my mom telling the story. Her general tone falls in between Martin Luther

King Jr.'s 'I Had a Dream' speech and a Joan Collins monologue on *Dynasty*. The point is, my mom's body and health has always been its own being, like a volcano that's dormant but needs to be watched, for all of my life. When I was a freshman in college, she told me she had a near death experience. She was home alone and had an insulin reaction that left her on the ground, unable to move. She was not able to reach her glucose tablets that would help regulate her sugar. She said she was slipping away, her body giving out, and was ready to fall into a diabetic coma.

'The only thing Jay, that kept me alive... was you,' she told me.

I sat there, silent.

'I said to myself, you got to stay alive for Jay. He's not ready for you to go. He's not ready.'

Hearing this at 19, I likely made a joke about drums, violins, and harps playing as background music as she spoke, against the flutter of doves' wings flapping towards a dark sky.

That's what it's like to know Carrie. She is dramatic, her own theatre department, is a little confusing at times, but also really funny and heartwarming too. I know now, how much trauma her body has gone through, and can see how her attitude or point-of-view helps her level with all of it. Two years ago, she stayed with Matthew and me in Brooklyn for about a week. One morning, at about 8 am, I was in the bathroom when I heard her call out for me.

'Jayyyyy...'

This wasn't a piercing yell. It sounded like it was taking all of her might for her to use her voice to get out sound. I ran out of the bathroom and saw her flailing on the couch. She was having an insulin reaction. I rushed to get Matthew, who looked like the closest thing I've ever seen to a deer-in-headlights. I ran to the refrigerator and grabbed her insulin. But wait, what the fuck was I doing? I didn't know how to administer insulin. What if I killed her? I didn't even know if her sugar was too high or low.

'I need to call 911,' I said.

As I was telling the operator what was happening, I looked down, and Carrie looked like a baby. She was smiling. She looked straight at me and seemed so, so happy. I looked directly into her eyes, and she looked into mine. I saw peace and what could even be described as bliss. The paramedics came within minutes, gave her a shot of something strong, and her blood-sugar started to stabilize as she was coming-to. She told the paramedics that she didn't want to go to the hospital, but I wasn't having it.

I sat with her in the back of the ambulance as it pulled onto the road. Carrie took her phone out and let out a gut-busting laugh.

'Hold on, Jay. I gotta take a selfie of this!'

September 18, 8:25 am

Last night, Leo asked if I'd come see him tomorrow, which is now today, instead of next week. I told him yes. Matthew and I had tentative plans today to celebrate, or pre-celebrate our wedding anniversary, which is on Monday, three days from today. We scrambled to find what it was we could do. A museum, maybe, a day trip to Beacon, but Beacon was sold out. After Leo asked me to come up, I thought of another plan for Matthew and myself. We'll rent a car the weekend of the 26th and spend the night in Nyack, the little balloon-festival town outside of NYC.

I asked Matthew if it was okay that I was going away this weekend. He, as always, had no objection. Leo's urgency in asking me to visit on a whim struck something in me. A kind of lust, yes, and a reminder of what I missed out on in my twenties while dating: the feeling of an ongoing interest from someone I was intimate with. Leo may also just not be too keen on fucking randoms right now, in times of Covid, so it makes sense that he'd ask to see me. During the beginning of the pandemic, I proposed to him that he and I become exclusive-esque sex partners (with the exception of Matthew). Maybe that idea bore into his brain, but maybe not. His thought processes can sometimes be hard to track.

I have other reasons for wanting this trip, too. There is something to Leo and something to our sex that is specific. He texted me last night that he was going to buy a box of donuts before I arrived at his place.

'...as a little treat for you to eat, without hands, off my dick.'

It's not humiliation that he presents me with. It's more like I am a willing prop for his fantasies: eating donuts off his dick, dressing up in a wrestling singlet, having him record me as he pumps cum in my mouth. He's playful, strange, and as he once told me *has a little bit of bully in him*. He's like that boy in Kindergarten, the one who would pull his pants down and expose himself to me. That sounds creepier than it's meant to. What I mean is–there's a melding of fantasy and reality here for me. Leo is a little bizarre; masculine in nature; rough-around-the-edges; a man with a boyish side. Sometimes it feels like we're both figuring ourselves out while exploring with one another and I hold that close, because there is safety in our friendship, and a curiosity in our bodies.

Sidenote, since I bought my Amtrak ticket last minute, there was only one type of accommodation left on the train. I purchased a small room, a *roomette* as they call it. My roomette will have two small beds, a window, a bathroom (or really just an open toilet), and a reading lamp. I'm going to pretend I am a Hitchcock blonde, in a tweed pencil-skirt, my mind filled with thoughts as I glance out onto the rolling hills and countryside.

4:45 pm

I realize that I am writing this lying down in a private room, traveling on a train, with plans to fuck someone other than my husband, but I'm starting to really believe that one should take part in unbridled pleasure. If we're fortunate enough to make room for it, then I think we should be smart enough to act upon it.

My thoughts swing back to what it was like to work at Homecoming Hotel, probably because I'm sitting here wearing an Oxford button down that was my go-to for a semi-professional wardrobe. I'd be so stressed and tied-up that I'd sit in the back office eating day-old pastries instead of taking time and having a proper meal. I would wait to go pee until it was almost an emergency. I'd never shut the office door, always having an ear perked to listen for heightened voices, ready to pop out at any moment to diffuse matters or a confrontation between Front Desk agents and guests.

It's been six months since I was furloughed. Earlier today, the GM requested to be a part of my network on LinkedIn. Is that a sign of what is to come: a final nail in the coffin and permanent closure of the hotel?

September 19, 9:40 am
New Paltz, NY

What is it that I need to be satisfied? Is it a push and pull of the heart? Is it a swim that goes beyond the shore, and I play with how far I can drift into the sea? I have moments while here with Leo where I miss Matthew, and my heart becomes heavy when I picture him going to bed alone. Thoughts and images of an abandoned child come to mind, and that hurt reminds me of how much I love him.

When Leo and I woke up this morning, my body was pressed against his. His arm was wrapped around my chest, his chest bringing warmth to my back. Our hips grinded against each other in circular motions, moving in sync.

5:56 pm

I am not the final say or even an authority of what it is to be Queer. I certainly have had my own notions of the many versions of love, what defines romanticism or friendship, and where my desire lies. Queerness, right at this moment, feels like it's sprawling. This afternoon, while wiggling a sex toy inside Leo, watching him while administering pleasure, I thought there are sides to myself that still need to be explored.

I don't mean to sound like *The Secret* and give a lesson in giving and gratitude but I thought, what if I put myself aside; what if I thought less of my own hunger? Would the reward of pleasing take some of my edge off? When I was playing with Leo's ass, when his legs were spread, his balls, and his anus and his taint were in my mouth, that feeling of consuming his whole body and not just part of it, made the ground feel solid. I wasn't waiting for anything but was simply satisfied to *have him* instead.

September 20

The train just departed from the Poughkeepsie station, heading back to NYC. Leo dropped me off and thanked me for the fun weekend. He most likely was referring to when I was on my knees, a donut was around his dick and smeared chocolate on my face. We may have agreed though, that at times it wasn't the sexiest experience, there was just so much chewing involved. I realized I never really say no to Leo, and it's never occurred to me to.

I'm glad I made the trip, as I always am. This is the third time I've visited since June, one of the few places I've traveled to since quarantine. Leo is a gracious host, makes eggs and toast and coffee every morning and weird fruit smoothies filled with Red Bull for snacks. He can still be a smart-ass, and I wonder how conscious he is that he makes my nostrils flare.

That morning, Leo asked me, 'Am I rude?'

'You straddle a fine line,' I said.

'That means yes.'

Moments earlier, Leo told me his back hurt and he thought he ought to try some planking exercises in an attempt to strengthen his core.

'Do you have a weak back? You always seem to be on your couch,' he said.

'I go running every day.'

'Oh right, yeah. Judging by your social media, all of your posts and stories are usually from the couch, so...'

The room turned silent.

He continued, 'Alright, well, I'm going to take Rudy out for a walk.'

Rudy is his dog, a German-Shepherd who stares at him for twenty minutes straight, like she's waiting to tell him a million things but can't because she's unable to speak.

I slid over to the edge of the couch and slipped my sneakers on. 'You know what, I'll go with you. I should get up and move. I don't want to just lay on the couch.'

That's when Leo asked if he was rude. He makes me sigh, smile, and roll my eyes at times, but I find that you just have to hit back a little if he starts to jab. He told me once that his humor and its intent to provoke was out of love. For me, it's like being pushed from behind, each time he pushes a bit harder. It's most effective when we're naked, but when we're clothed, it can feel coarse. And then... I find myself feeling sympathy for Leo. He tells me stories about being ignored or pushed away from guys after they've been together. I know that's not an uncommon thing, especially when dating, being gay, being on apps... but it shows that Leo wants more and everyone should at least be given the chance to have that.

September 21

Today is my one-year wedding anniversary. Last night, guilt swirled inside me for the hardships I've put Matthew through and for hurtful things that I've said. I don't think I've been the same source of security for him as he has been for me, though I don't like apologizing *too* much. I regret when I become overly apologetic and call myself 'crazy.' I, like my mother, may operate my own rollercoaster, but I'm not crazy. Besides, I'm the only one who calls myself that. Matthew never would.

I talked to Matthew last night about how I feel anxious since we don't have a solid plan for the future. We've never discussed buying a home, moving out of NYC, if we're going to have children, if we should invest in property, or even if we'd like a dog or cat, or what are additional ways we could bring in income, or if we're ever planning on switching careers, and where would we do that and when. There were so many questions, and I started to feel anxious and it felt like I was floating. I know I said that I wasn't looking to have a plan, but I still would like to talk about one, even if we reject it together.

'Maybe it's time we start discussing these things,' he said.

He was right. I wonder what we'll do. Will we buy property when we have the money, possibly outside of the city, possibly up north? As I write this, I can hear Bernard Herrmann playing. Matthew and I are walking through an old house, with creaky wood floors and an oak staircase.

September 22

I spoke to my mom today. She told me that she received good news from her doctor. She had gone to get a biopsy, but instead, her doctor only performed an ultrasound. She and him both took a look at what he called abnormal cells. As a fix, she is going to have the cells, or lesions, 'burned out.' For the procedure, she'll be admitted as an outpatient at a hospital in Miami. From there, they can take what is extracted and then perform a biopsy. The doctor told her that the surgery must be done whether there is cancer or not. Even if there is cancer, which they don't think there is, there's no sign that it's spread.

'Today was a good day,' she said.

It's a small reminder of hope. Yeah, Death is ultimately coming but maybe not so soon.

It has been a while since time afforded me something to look forward to. Every day on the news, things seem to be getting worse. The US just hit 200,000 deaths due to Covid-19. The Repubican Party may appoint a Supreme Court judge who is anti-abortion, and maybe anti-everything. NYC, as a whole, feels empty-ish and has an uncomfortable, quiet intensity in the air. I'm sure many cities and towns at the moment share the same feeling. It's like there's not much to connect to, not many people to connect to, not yet anyways. There is a looming question of what the winter will bring in regards to the virus. There is an indecisive air of what will come.

After speaking with my mom, I took a walk to Industry City (a gentrified, mostly unwelcomed tech-heavy playground for artisan-based businesses in Sunset Park, Brooklyn). It looked like an apocalyptic playground where the only survivors were a few 35-year-old hipsters. I sat there, at a table, on the edge of a miniature golf-course. Some guy sitting across from me, with a Coke can and straw, might have been cruising me. His soft eyes and straw at least told me that he wasn't straight. He stared at me as I jotted down words in my notebook. Maybe he wondered what I was writing about. *Yes, I'm writing about you*, I thought.

September 23

Matthew told me that an artist named Guy, in Detroit, wants to draw us. Whenever an artist asks to draw a couple, there's at least an implication that they'd like for the couple to engage in an act of sex.

This, I am for.

I DM'd Guy, mentioned Matthew told me about him, and he said he was looking forward to us posing. Then he asked if his husband, Paul, could sit in and watch. Of course, I said yes. He shared that Matthew has plans to draw him and his husband as well, as a trade-off.

'Would you like to sit in and watch the session?' he asked.

I, of course, said yes.

I told him that I found there to be something hot and communal when two couples share and interact.

I TOTALLY AGREE, Guy wrote in all-caps. He sent me the link to his husband's profile and suggested we say hello or chat to get more comfortable with each other.

I've been intrigued for a couple years by the number four, at the thought of two couples being together. As I told my new voyeur-loving friend, Guy, that finding another couple to play with is hard to come by, he said he and his husband 'like to involve each other' but are not 'all the way open' and only like to 'show off.' It was then that I started my investigational research. I lurked both of their Instagram pages and checked dates. It looked like they were married this past summer, and have been together for about two-and-a-half years.

I've been in their place before. Exploring desire while keeping your loved one in the picture. I mean, maybe they truly do enjoy being a monogamous, voyeuristic couple. They could be on Chatterbate or Cam4Cam right now giving the performance of a lifetime and be totally content. Afterall, I don't like to impose my past experiences on someone else or on someone else's relationship. Though, the insistence of involving one's partner when opening a marriage, combined with only having a two-and-a-half year history together feels so familiar. Looking back, I could have been more honest with what and whom I desired in the past. I was scared to say to Matthew, I want to have sex with this person, just by myself. I feared I would be hurting him, so I tip-toed around the truth.

Alas, it's helpful to know information about others so I can gauge how they operate. Still, this in no way interrupts my appetite. What I would like is to share with this couple, and for the four of us to share our sex together, even if its only virtually. I want us to watch each other while we suck our partner's cock. I want there to be hunger on both sides. I want them to *want* to show Matthew and me their sex. It's not just about voyeurism. I want a meshing of our legs, and hands on the back of our necks. I want magnetism; a tiny ache, even if it's all just in our imaginations.

I took a lot of notes.

September 24

I keep thinking of time capsules and the urgency I have to make them. This morning, I organized 200 family photos from Kingston, Jamaica and New York City, spanning over 80 years. I need there to be visual evidence of where my family came from, of their once Brown skin that eventually passed as white during the first half of the 20th century. If I could take everything that I've gathered: pictures, documents, marriage certificates and place them in an album, then it will feel solid; like the past did exist and I am a product of it.

I bought two *New York Times* back in April, or was it May, maybe it was June, as evidence of what was happening in the country. On the cover was the headline that read 100,000 lives in the US were lost due to Covid-19.

Today, there are over 200,000 dead.

I saved the protest signs I made over the summer for Black Lives Matter marches. One is of Audre Lorde's poem, 'Power.' Yesterday, I went to a Studio 54 Exhibition at the Brooklyn Museum, a time capsule of New York City of the late 1970s. NYC today, in September 2020, bears some resemblance; mass gatherings demanding social justice; crime increasing on the subways; the city allegedly going broke.

I don't want to go through all of my life needing to save every moment. That sounds too tiring, even for me. There is something about now, right now, during these months, of this year, today, that needs to be recorded. What is happening *now* needs to be read fifty, sixty, seventy... even one, two, or three years from today.

This afternoon, I said to my therapist that my voice doesn't matter that much. What I have to say isn't necessarily important but if it can be reflective of another's experience, or if it's at all reflective of the time we're in, then that's all I want my time capsule to be.

September 25

I suppose, you could say, I've had a problem with excess. If I receive something that I like, I only want more of it until I can ingest it no more. It's like there is a chip or circuit missing in my brain that says, *this is enough*. The last time I drank was on March 10th, 2020. Alcohol was not always a substance of choice. For about four years, Adderall was all that I preferred. I loved a stimulant. It felt like my body was finally catching up with my brain. The euphoria from a stimulant, specifically Adderall, brought a feeling of serenity, possibility, and accomplishment that wouldn't last too long but long enough for me to want to recreate the feeling over and over.

I became savvy to my habits early on. For half of the week, I would imbibe/ingest. Three full days on Adderall, very limited sleep, not much food (much less healthy food), and no exercise. Then, I would spend the other half of the week being super healthy: eating greens, juicing, running five to six miles a day to make sure I sweat out the toxins I had put in my body. In hindsight, this wasn't the worst habit to have, but it feels like being on a hamster wheel. I moved to New York in 2008 and because I didn't have an Adderall contact, and didn't want one, I stopped cold turkey. Since then, I've maybe taken it once a year, but so much time has passed, that I no longer feel the pull or dependency of needing it.

In 2012, I started drinking whiskey and consciously made it my drink of choice, only drinking it straight. I liked that you could drink it in small amounts, quickly get rid of it, then pour another small amount, make it disappear, and pour another, as if the previous pour didn't exist. This was around the time that I was dating Victor (the one who I picked up and fell in love with from the local bodega). We, and sometimes just me, would hang out at bars after work. I usually worked the evening shift at the hotel, so I was out by about midnight. From 12 until 4 am was drinking time, where you would sit with other people who worked late shifts in hospitality. By 2017, I regulated things a bit but not necessarily for the better. I would drink (and smoke half a pack of American Spirits) once or twice a week, sometimes on my day off (though not always). I would start drinking around 7 pm. I only drank alone, sitting on our back porch while Matthew watched TV or painted, before he eventually went to bed. I would start at 7, always having a pen and notebook with me as I sipped. I began the night by writing down thoughts and ideas. I'd have my headphones with me, feeling nostalgic, listening to songs usually released between 2000–2007 (genre being electroclash or rap), and I'd light up a cigarette every 15–20 minutes.

From there, I would tumble into the past, into my thoughts and memories while the liquor took effect. I'd go deeper and deeper into a well, the same songs on repeat, until it was 6 am. Then, I'd go inside, sit on the couch, and tell myself I'll get ready for bed... in just a minute. Matthew would find me an hour later, slumped over and slurring, and I'd walk with him to the bedroom, and he'd tuck me in.

Honestly, that was the part that wasn't so bad. It was the next morning that felt treacherous.

I'd wake up, and my body felt like lead had been poured inside.

I said I wouldn't do this again.

This is when I wanted the night before out of my system, this pollution that I poured in. I'd hobble to the bathroom, get on my knees, my face barely above the toilet, and I'd shove two fingers down my throat. This felt rougher on my stomach than it did my esophagus because I hadn't eaten dinner the night before so nothing wanted to come out. Eventually when the mixture of water, whiskey, and bile left my body, the aftertaste was another reminder that I couldn't control how much I drank.

I knew all of this would eventually take a toll on my body. By now, I was 36 years old. If I kept this up, what would happen by the time I reached fifty? And yes, for a while, I tried the whole 'moderate your drinking' approach. I'll tell you this: I've had very smart people with psychology degrees suggest this is what I need to work on, this is what I needed to do; to learn how to regulate. But they don't know what it's like to not have an off switch, or maybe they do, I shouldn't assume. I tried really hard, for a long time to change — to be like the rest of people who seemingly had healthy drinking habits — but I couldn't.

When it became real and apparent that NYC was going into a kind of lockdown due to the pandemic, I thought, *this is my chance*. I'm not going to have the daily stresses of work. I'm not going to have to deal with being social or having to go to a social gathering where there'd be drinking (even though I did most of it when I was alone). Now is my chance to stop. So, I did.

The first three weeks were hard, and it wasn't because I was craving alcohol. It felt like I was saying goodbye to someone, like I was leaving a relationship of habit, one that I kept going back to for years and years. While I acknowledge my tumultuous or intense relationship with alcohol or substances, I cannot help but wonder if I'll abstain forever. I don't forget what it's like to not have an off switch. It's dreamy to be honest. It's like everything melts and then I'm floating comfortably downstream. There's also a challenge that I've come to enjoy in being sober; time passing feels like endurance.

But then I do wonder, is the problem not the substance, but the self-punishment? And can it be harmful to have a lifetime of no; to exist forever in your own self-made restriction; to never try to re-explore a past relationship or habit? The memories and consequences of getting too fucked-up (and the harshness I've treated my body with) don't leave me. My nature of questioning the absolute does not go away either and I don't think it ever will.

At one time, drinking may have been a kind of suppression for me, drowning out certain feelings and fears. I do not, however, think that is what it became. What if imbibing is a way of peeling off the rigidity of everyday life; a ritual and a potion that makes the dullness of day-to-day life disappear? When I think of the root of why I wanted to become lost, what this need was or is to ingest and be elsewhere for a while, I'm reminded of how much we have to tuck away, every day, and how many urges and desires we know are there but we put to rest every day, every hour: while we sit on the train; are stuck in traffic; while we watch television; while we chit-chat with acquaintances; while we eat a boring dinner; while we glance away from strangers, before we wonder what their flesh looks and feels like under their clothes.

September 26

I think I care more about recording my experiences than I do about recording my queerness, which yes, is a part of my experience. I was thinking about my own contrasts or differences between myself and other gay men, in 2020, and how social media is used in ways in which I do not relate. I would not post a picture of my face with a rainbow behind me and a caption that reads 'This is what Queer looks like'. The intent may be harmless, as Queer is an umbrella term, but it feels too bold to define Queer, to attach it too tightly. Besides, I think the birth of a flag or slogan has weight and importance and can be useful during a political fight. Sooner than later though, there's an overreliance, a laziness, a danger in attaching identity with a symbol that was created to disrupt. What was once pride and resistance can disintegrate into a prop for a photo op.

I certainly wouldn't assume to use my face as a poster child for queerness because I am only a stitch in a sprawling fabric. I can, however, describe what Queer feels like: soft dark hair lining a wrist, the smell of skin, the smell of one's wrist. The immediacy of a first touch. The coating of saliva on one's mouth. The roughness of stubble around lips; lips that may taste like nothing, like skin.

My queerness is not so much what is in me; it is in the detail I see in another.

September 27

Sunday, to me, feels melancholy, and today I'd like for that feeling to pass. No, I don't feel that way because tomorrow is Monday or whatever that corny thing is that people say. It's the same feeling I get around 5 pm or near dusk. It's like time stops for a few moments, or hours. For some, that may be a feeling they look forward to and hold on to. Me, it makes me feel lonely, like there's a chance that I may not talk to anyone, ever again. I guess, on quiet days, I'm reminded that I look for connection. Maybe connection isn't the right word... but exploration is.

On Sundays, and at dusk, the want for something new and undiscovered sits heavier on my chest than usual. Someone once told me that when I want something, I want it right then. I'm not exactly friendly with time and waiting, either. I do believe we get what we want, but there is a trade because there has to be. What you want will be delivered to you, but you must wait to receive, and with waiting comes the strong possibility of suffering.

September 28, 6:10 am

I cannot help but fly into a sort of retrospective this morning and think of what was. My mom is arriving at the hospital now, for surgery and a biopsy that starts prepping at 6 am. I woke up at 4:54 and couldn't go back to sleep. I'd like to go back to sleep, but I have too much energy, nervous energy I guess.

When I get a restless, anxious energy, it needs to be kneaded through. As I see it, at this moment, I could either jerk off or write... or maybe both. I remember a certain Sunday (my day of unrest), in the late nineties, in the house I grew up in. I was fifteen and procrastinating doing my homework, which was due the next day. The afternoon was passing by as I was watching a tornado disaster movie with Devon Sawa. I laid on the floor with one of those headrest pillows with the little arms on the left and right side and a blanket draped over myself. I masturbated, stroking myself for hours. This might have been the first time I edged. Maybe that's what Sundays should be used for. *Sunday, a Day of Edge*. I wanted to fuck or at least have Devon Sawa under the blanket with me. He had that Corey Haim quality to him, a bit of a wild boy quality that still to this day I crave. I laid there jerking, feeling sloppy and balmy, my balls aching.

I don't blame myself, per se, for withholding my queerness as a teenager. There was so much buried, so deep. Where my 'story' takes a detour from the normative gay-teenage-boy-in-suburbia narrative, begins with my body. My body, during puberty, seemed to, I guess you could say, interrupt itself. My voice started to change around the age of fourteen, the average age when boys' voices change, but it didn't deepen as much as it could have. It had a raspy, brittle tone. It was at an in-between stage, between a child's and a man's voice. The thing that gave me trouble is that I could not project it in its natural state. If I tried, really dug, a much deeper, baritone sound would come out. At the time, this seemed unnatural. Why would I have to consciously speak from my gut? Why wasn't this happening on its own?

Around the same time as this 'non-dropping' of my voice, I began to develop gynecomastia, a condition when men develop 'extra' breast tissue. I always, always wore an undershirt, because of the small, chewed-up bubble-gum like lumps underneath my nipples. No matter how hot the Florida sun was, I never went out in public with only one T-shirt. I read that many boys experience this during puberty as a result of changing hormones. I also read that it will eventually go away on its own. So, I waited. Time passed, and then a year passed, another year, and another after that, but the lumps never went away.

So now, at this point, I'm 21. I had not yet begun to explore my queerness with other men, my voice literally felt stifled, and no one, I mean no one ever saw me without a shirt. It's as though puberty began but didn't bother to finish. What could I do? Well, I decided to push through, to finish what was started.

I don't want to go on another complete tangent here but, in my youth, I was known for prank phone calls. I could put on any voice; I had the ability to deepen my voice, it just wouldn't stick. I've pranked phone-called people as a man, as a woman, as a radio show announcer, and as a doctor named Dr. Chilton (yes, as in *The Silence of the Lambs*). I've done it all and I learned that the key to a successful prank is never to break. The harder that those around me laughed, their hands covering their mouths, faces turning red with tears in their eyes, the more I could tune in and concentrate. I had practice experimenting with other voices, including expanding and deepening the one I had.

I decided, the summer before my junior year of college, that I was going to permanently change my voice. I told my family and close friends what I was going to do, and that I'll sound different from now on. I did my research, probably on AOL 3.0 or Netscape at the time. I read that once vocal chords expand, they stay that way. The first week using my new voice felt a little like an identity crisis. To hear what sounds like someone else coming out of your mouth is a peculiar thing. This took both practice and commitment. I consciously pushed my voice through using my stomach and diaphragm as my base, instead of my throat and nose. Within a week, I had a new sound and my old voice was a thing of the past.

My voice was changed, and now, I wanted to feel comfortable taking my shirt off in front of people. I found a website that centered around gynecomastia and rummaged through its message boards. There were a lot of men out there like me. I noticed that when someone did get the surgery to remove the 'extra' breast tissue, they soon became absent on the message boards. It might have been a common understanding among the men that after someone had the surgery, they were on the other side now, and moved on. I wanted to be on the other side. I found a plastic surgeon who specialized in that type of surgery in Orlando, FL, where I was attending school. I read all of the surgeon's reviews as I wanted to feel confident and sure. The surgery cost $5,000, wasn't covered by insurance, and was considered a cosmetic procedure. I told my parents that I wanted to do it. I don't think it was that much of a shock for my mom. She was aware of my self-consciousness.

'It's not that noticeable,' she'd say.

Her and my dad, who were not the best of friends at the time, split the cost of the surgery. The recovery was pretty minimal. I had to wear bandage compressions for about six weeks. I was also prescribed a fairly large dose of Percocet, which yes, I did abuse. Pills, drinks, food... anything that is digestible, I will dutifully consume.

Looking back, I wonder how or why my body developed like it did. Was it a psychological thing? Did I mentally block my body from developing? Seeing myself as an Intersex person, while intriguing, is too much of a stretch to give more than a few seconds of thought. Does it matter? Is there a point in wondering? It's kind of like all contemplation; there isn't one answer. So, I better be okay with the past existing in a gray area. I've learned to live with the gray.

What was difficult was that I felt like I held a secret. When I moved to New York and started dating, no one knew that I was also a virgin, closeted, and had surgery and deepened my own voice only a couple years prior. I wasn't ready to tell them, either. I wonder what those boys saw, what history they made up for me since I was reluctant to share my own.

September 30

I was aware all of yesterday that at 6:30 pm, Matthew and I were to be on a Zoom call, posing nude for Guy, the Detroit artist, and his husband Paul. We agreed that Matthew was to draw them as well and we'd alternate taking turns. Matthew and I would choose our poses and then they would mimic ours. What I liked about this scenario was the sexual aspect of it, obviously. Like I said before, I've been intrigued by the number four.

Here's the thing. I am not a model, and I don't typically pose nude. I have in the past, but that was just for Matthew. Matthew runs a Queer figure drawing group called 'Desirable Dudes,' same name as his zine. I know he appreciates art depicting the male human form. He celebrates the body, and he likes the community that this group has helped create. He more than likes it; he values it. There's another element to this, though. Public nudity may be Matthew's kink: posing for an audience, becoming hard for a photographer, having his body drawn and then displayed online. There's a showman in Matthew; an appreciation for performance and public affection.

When we first started dating, I didn't get it. Does he just want to be in porn, I wondered.

And no, I don't think he wants to be a porn star, although I don't think he would 100 percent refuse it, either. There's an exhibitionist inside of him, and once I became secure enough in our relationship, I pushed for him to explore it. It's his and I want him to have that. And while I enjoy thoughts of sex on a community-type group level, I've always been too self-conscious of my own body to want to show it publicly. I didn't realize how prevalent that self-consciousness still was until about ten minutes before our Zoom call.

I decided before we started this drawing session that I wanted to begin by wearing a wrestling singlet. Leo had given me one when I was in New Paltz. I wonder if he'd be happy, or a bit jealous if he knew of its current use. Guy suggested that Matthew wear a jock-strap to compliment my singlet for a faux 'locker room' scene. Does this sound cliché? Sure. Still, there's a kitsch to it that I welcome. By now, it was 6:15 pm. In the bathroom, I slipped on a silver cockring and adjusted my singlet, making sure it fit correctly.

Do I find all of this sex-gear pretty hot? Yeah, but there's more to it. I'm trying to conceal part of my body. The singlet fits very tight and the effect is me looking a bit thinner than I actually am. It smooths out any bulges around my sides. The cockring, when I'm hard, causes me to swell, appearing bigger than I actually am. I hate that these stereotypical insecurities plague me. If I do this or that, I'll look a little bit thinner and my cock a little bit bigger. None of this even matters since I'd be naked eventually, anyways. It was 6:20. I was grappling to try and feel secure and relaxed and I felt neither. Matthew was in the living room, setting up his iPad on the tripod.

'We have like what, five minutes?' I asked.

'Yea, I told them 6:30.'

'So, here's the thing. I don't normally do this. This isn't like my thing,' I said.

Matthew had a slightly bewildered look in his eye. I am more than familiar with this look, as I am the one who causes it.

I continued, 'I'm not, like, totally comfortable with my body. Also, just the public aspect of this, when the drawings are put online, like, it's not my thing. I think I'm having a moment or something. I need a few minutes.'

Matthew looked concerned.

'I just, I don't fuckin' know. I'm not a model. I don't do this. This is your thing,' I said.

'We can cancel.'

'No, don't.'

'I'll tell them my work meeting ran late; I can cancel.'

'No, Matthew, you're not hearing me. I don't want to cancel. I want to do this. I try to do things that I'm not comfortable with. I think that's why I do them. I just, um...'

'It's okay, I'll cancel,' Matthew said.

'No, fuck, Matthew. You're not listening to me. I don't want you to cancel. You're like putting gasoline on my anxiety right now.'

Matthew's eyes were red and starting to water.

He said, 'I'm sorry I made you do this. I don't want you to feel uncomfortable.'

This is when I calm down and withdraw my defenses. There's a sweetness or an innocence to Matthew that causes me to come out of myself. I put my arm around him.

'You're fine, Matthew. I'm sorry. I don't want to make you feel bad. When I get like this, sometimes I just need a few minutes. Sometimes, I just want you to be the one to recognize that.'

He nods.

'So, write to them and tell them we'll start at 7.'

It was kind of cute that Guy and Paul matched their outfits to mine and Matthew's. Paul wore a singlet and Guy a jockstrap. I saw that Guy has a 'perfect' body. He is at least 6 foot tall, has all lean muscle, no body fat, has what might be a 6-pack, his face is handsome and chiseled, with a full head of naturally highlighted hair. It's almost too much, like a walking Ken doll, which is usually not my thing. I've never been that attracted to the blond-haired, washboard abs type. What I did notice about Guy though, when I heard him speak when we virtually met, is that there's a strictness to him. He was very aware of times and schedules. His words and expressions had a formal tone to them, a properness. Paul, his husband, on the other hand, seemed like the more personable one. He's in his early forties and smiles a lot, and cracked a couple of jokes. His body is broader, thicker, hairier, more mature than Guy's. He possesses a charmful quality: an ability to disarm.

By the time we started our first pose, I was at ease. Wearing my singlet, I found that I enjoyed staying in one position for ten minutes at a time. I liked the rigidity. Beads of sweat formed at the top of my head. As discussed, Guy and Paul recreated our pose after our ten minutes were up. Matthew sketched away, as did I. Well, I don't really sketch as much as I draw obscure images with pastel crayons. It's like a stream-of-consciousness thing; I draw whatever shapes I see in the moment.

Next, I stripped off my singlet. By this point, my attitude was 'fuck it.' When an atmosphere turns sexual, a calm washes over me. My instincts were telling me that this session was no longer going to be demure. When I looked over to Matthew's iPad, I saw that Guy and Paul were now naked. The iPad was a few feet from us, a bit too far for me to see in great detail. I saw Guy adjusting a cockring, attached to a cock that when swelled, looked like a snake still digesting its food. I planted myself down on the desk chair we were using as a prop, my back to the screen. Matthew laid his dick over my hand, only a few inches from my face. It was already growing.

Third pose. I climbed onto the back of our couch, spread my legs, hand over my dick. Matthew sat upright in front of me. It looked both pornographic and presidential. I was done holding back. I looked into the camera and kept my body solid, unmoving except for the palm of my hand. I began to caress myself. Guy, I saw, was getting hard. His sketchbook was still in his hand. Paul was openly stroking. A couple minutes passed, and Matthew broke his pose, turning his head just a little. He started licking the top of my dick, now rock hard. Guy laid his sketchbook down. The four of us began to jerk off together. I was still straddled across the back of the couch.

For what was to be our final pose, Matthew sat on the couch's arm. His legs open, his dick still fully hard. I lay on my side, my head inches from his cock. I twisted my body, and put one leg across the back of the couch in a contortionist-style pose.

'Are you going to be okay posing like that?' Paul asked.

Confidently, I smiled and nodded. Guy began to sketch but not for long.

I turned my head and put Matthew's swelled cock against my lips. I let it get wet and smack against my mouth. I made sucking and kissing sounds as I ran my lips over his shaft. Guy and Paul watched us, jerking their cocks. All sketchbooks are down. Matthew and I sit side-by-side, the four of us now facing each other. Paul began to moan. Matthew stood up, bent down on his knees, and started to suck me off. Paul, with his back to the camera, was now on his knees with Guy in his mouth. Paul and Matthew's heads bobbed up and down. I looked into the screen. Guy and I watched each other getting pleasured. This, I realize, is where I wanted this to go. Looking at Guy, sharing a moment with him; a moment filled with power, warmth, and pleasure.

The next day, Guy kept in touch via a group chat. He sent the three of us memes about last night's disastrous Presidential Debate, the one where Trump told the Proud Boys to stand-by. I think one of the memes read, 'After last night, America deserves another Chris Evans dick pic.' Not totally my sense of humor, but cute I guess. I appreciate the correspondence. I'd like for this to continue, whatever it is; the openness of it all, the involvement of four.

That's a cool trend

OCTOBER 2020 PART I

October 1, 9:00 am

I woke up to an email this morning from Homecoming Hotel, or rather from the General Manager. The hotel will not be reopening. The email also said the news is 'soul-crushing' and that they did everything in their power to stay open. Well, I for one feel like fucking celebrating. Yes, I have to be mindful of money and all that, but who the fuck cares? I almost want a disco ball to fall from the ceiling and Donna Summer's 'I Feel Love' to start playing in a room full of mirrors.

I don't have to go back there. I don't have to deal with fucking asshole guests and customers treating staff like shit just because they think they're checking into a 'cool' hotel. Fuck that. I know I sound especially angry right now, and yes, I am an angsty man but unless you've worked in customer service, you have no idea how horrid human beings can be.

Homecoming Hotel did feature a lot of art, artists, and held Queer community driven events. That's all great and awesome that they provided the space. But they didn't *make* that art, they didn't *make* those artists, and the events weren't born from their walls. It goes without saying that I enjoyed the teamwork I experienced there with my coworkers. I'll hold that fondly in my memories. But fuck those Wall Street bros in Patagonia sweater vests getting wasted in the lobby at 5 pm. Fuck the asshole men and women coming straight from LAX, who'd leave their luggage sitting at the entryway, walking up to the desk and absolutely refusing to look the staff in the eye, half-mumbling their name at reception. Fuck the mold in the rooms, the TVs that never worked, the defective air conditioners. Fuck the room service trays that would be left in the hallways for twelve hours at a time.

I don't have to hear the bullshit talks about how 'not corporate' the company is despite hearing about their cover-ups of sexual harassment, homophobia, and racist complaints and allegations. I don't ever have to hear the words 'On Brand' again. I no longer have to judge prospective new hires by how "non-conformist" they appear. I don't have to be told that I should feel grateful to be a part of a company. I'm relieved that I don't have to feel the hypocrisy of going back there because I need a paycheck and insurance during a pandemic. The truth is, even if they stayed open, I wouldn't go back because I have no interest in mending Homecoming's brokenness. I no longer have it in me to be a part of its progressive facade.

In the meantime, I wonder if they're going to offer some sort of severance. I would think they would. I'm not going to tell anyone besides Matthew that I'm not going back to work, at least for a little while. People sometimes like to make plans for you, and I'm not looking for that. I know I need to make a Plan B and eventually I will have to find employment. I can not work for now though, that's for sure. Besides, I may not even have a choice. I'm going to see how far I can get, maybe finish out 2020 as I'm doing now. Wake up, write, apply for a job or two, watch a Brian De Palma movie, which has become my thing. I'll see how much unemployment I can save and how far I can sensibly go. Maybe I can actually go somewhere during the holidays, if there's not another Covid spike and lockdown. I could go with Matthew to Oregon to see his family, and the rocky cliff mountain shore lined with sea lions. I could do another trip to Florida, spend a holiday with my mom.

I keep taking moments of pause, trying to think of reasons why I shouldn't feel relief. I can't think of any.

October 2, 8:51 am

It's weird sometimes during this pandemic how one spends almost all of their time indoors, with seemingly not much happening, yet we are filled with outside narratives that are affecting our inner lives. At 5:30 this morning, I woke up to a text saying that Donald Trump and Melania tested positive for Covid-19. By 8 am, the internet was exploding.

Some people are laughing at him, and writing that they hope he dies. I don't damn their honesty. A friend of mine, who I haven't seen in years, but have kept in touch with via social media, posted that he doesn't feel sorry for Trump. He has every reason not to; his mother died of Covid-19. I follow a photographer who is HIV-positive, and he posted that we must remember that illness is not a punishment. My gut reaction when I heard that Trump tested positive was to post that he deserved it, but I too, do not feel that illness is a punishment and certainly not for the 205,000+ Americans who have died from Covid. If anything, rather than Trump *deserving* the illness, I see it more as a cause and effect. If you downplay the virus for months and do not follow health guidelines, well, this is what happens. Emotions aside, and feelings about Trump removed, this is pretty matter-of-fact.

11:59 am

Tucked within the non-stop 'Trump Tested Positive for Covid-19' news, another newsworthy headline has emerged.

ACTOR ATTACKED ON UPPER WEST SIDE: Rick Moranis sucker-punched on the street

I hope that we're not conditioned enough to forget that we're living inside absurdist theater.

October 3

It's a tricky sort of time right now. On one end, there is an opening where a new future, new possibilities (as a result of the pandemic) has emerged. New chances, new career, new people. But how am I going to find these things, especially when Covid continues to be part of the narrative? First I have to ask myself what I want, and I'll start with what I want for Matthew and me. If we're going to continue to have an open marriage, what's the best way of doing that, especially now?

If I went back to the apps, which seems counterproductive during quarantine, which ones would I use? I have an account with Squirt, but I don't know if that's for the best. I don't regret my experiences while on it, but I don't necessarily wish to repeat them either. It is a site that caters to public sex and voyeurism, but it's also a breeding ground, some pun intended, for closeted married men. So, that leaves a couple of options. There is Grindr, but the thought of it leaves me with a washed out, uneasy feeling. No disrespect to anyone on it, but it feels very 'Chelsea,' and no disrespect to Chelsea boys but let's be honest, I don't think they're hopping over any fences to get to me either. There's Scruff, the site where Matthew and I met. The gays on that site are a little hairier, or organic, you could say but I also heard they now have some fucked up censorship laws that I'm not trying to be a part of. Plus, if I do sign up, I should be realistic with myself; seeking what you want vs. what you get is not always in alignment. Fact is, I'm 37 and married, and I'm not seeking a 22-year-old obsessed with Kim Petras, who spends his days at outdoor dining ordering well drinks. Again, no disrespect to 22-year-olds who love Kim Petras and well drinks.

Maybe I'm just nervous. Nervous that if I don't fulfill certain wants of mine, I'll turn into someone who I met last January.

JANUARY 2020

AN OLD COWORKER of mine, Holly, had an opening party for a bougie hipster-type hotel in Kingston, NY. She was the General Manager. The owner was a man whose real name was Leopard. Leopard was a very good looking bro-dude. He wore cowboy hats, and walked with his legs spread wide, and in general looked like a douche. He did have charm though. I sat with him at the bar and he spoke about being a hotelier and designer, and what he believed made a brand successful. He stared into my eyes very deeply the whole time. He never broke eye contact, not once. Maybe he learned that trick from *The Art of the Deal*, who knows.

There was a couple there at the party; the only other gay people there besides me. Upstate may have its pockets of hip, but it's not cosmopolitan. One half of the couple was probably in his early fifties. He had a shaved head and wore a dangly earring. I remember he spoke *a lot* about The Cure and Culture Club. His husband (I don't remember either one of their names) was about ten years younger. He was sort of loud, sort of drunk, and was kooky like he could be on his own planet. Of course, I made friends with them.

After a few rounds of drinks, we made our way to the lounge, which was a living room area with a record player, lots of Native American motifs (which, combined with the overall cowboy aesthetic was not the most enlightened design choice; come on Leopard), and a fireplace which was pretty nice and cozy, especially in January.

Sitting next to me on the brown leather couch, the kooky one said, 'Do you want to make out?'

It was a bold question as his husband was in earshot. I don't know what type of marriage they had or what was their norm. It wasn't any of my business.

I nodded, yes, and not because I was particularly attracted to him. I was attracted to the question and the bluntness in which it was asked. He got up from the couch and started walking towards the hallway that led to the bathrooms. I looked over and saw that his husband was preoccupied. He was heavily engaged in a conversation about Chris Cornell. I let twenty seconds pass. I got up and walked toward the bathroom. When I turned down the hallway, I saw him standing in its center. Not in the bathroom, but standing there in the middle of the hall. I walked up to him, expecting him to take a lead into the bathroom, but he did not. He kissed me, hard, in the open. He pressed his mouth against mine, his tongue shoved down my throat.

'Why don't we... go in here,' I said.

I took a few steps towards the bathroom and he followed. I locked the door behind us. We kissed and groped, and I could feel his eagerness in his lips and palms. The taste of someone new is always nice. His sense of urgency caused me to pull back. A couple minutes later, our PG-13 rendezvous was finished, and we returned to our couch in the lounge. People were laughing and drinking. Someone was talking about Stevie Nicks, and talk still lingered about Chris Cornell.

Guests began leaving the party, dispersing back to their hotel rooms around 2 am. The rooms weren't typical hotel rooms. They were luxury rooms nestled inside luxury cabins. They were enormous too, with brass lined claw-tubs big enough to drown in. Next to the tub was a window that nearly took up the entire wall. When the snow fell, it looked like film playing in reverse. If you stared at it long enough, you couldn't tell if the snow was rising or falling. It turns out that the couple was not only staying in the same cabin as me, but their room was right below mine.

Twenty minutes after we said our goodbyes, there was a knock on my door. It was him, the kooky one. I knew he was going to be back. We didn't say much, if anything at all. He came into the room, with the same hungry look in his eyes, and walked toward me as I slowly backed up. I sat on the foot of the bed and unbuckled my pants. I pulled my jeans and underwear down to my ankles. He got on his knees, taking me in his mouth, and started sucking. I lay back, and closed my eyes. The room was spinning; I drank a lot of whiskey that night, along with a fair amount of edibles. I let him suck as long as I could, feeling the warmth of his mouth, the rapidness of his head bobbing and turning. When I came, I came in his mouth, because I knew that he was going to swallow.

He stood up and said, 'Maybe I can come back in a little bit. I told him (the husband) that I just went to get something from the car. I could be back soon. We could take a long, hot bath...'

'Oh, I, I'm actually pretty tired. I need to sleep soon,' I said.

'I know what can make you tired.'

'Yea, well... that sounds fun. I'm just really tired. I'm probably going to go right to bed.'

He was looking at me, eyes still aflame.

He said, 'My room is right below yours. When you're ready, knock three times on the floor. I'll know it's you.'

I didn't know what to say. I didn't want to be rude and offend him, but he didn't seem to be hearing me.

'If I'm up, then I will,' I said.

I walked him to the door. As he walked down the stairs, he glanced up at me, giving me 'the look.' I flashed a polite smile back.

By now, it was past 3. I stripped off my clothes, turned off the lights, and finally climbed into bed. But I couldn't fall asleep. I thought about how when he was leaving, and I was locking the door, I had to push against it with my shoulder to make sure it shut. I had to make sure I heard the door click before I locked it and still, I wasn't positive that it was locked. I thought of what Holly told me earlier when she was telling me about the hotel: the wood they used for the doors was warped because it was antique wood. Thus, they were having trouble staying closed. I laid there, thinking about the door, wondering if it was in fact locked. That's when I heard footsteps. Someone was coming up the stairs.

I listened to the footsteps getting closer. I threw the covers off of the bed, and grabbed the metallic cylinder-shaped nightstand next to the bed. I placed it directly in front of the door. If anyone tries to get in, the second they walk in, they'll trip over the stand. If anything, it'll give me time to decide what to do next. I peeked at the bottom of the door, where a sliver of light was coming through. Someone was standing there. I could see the shadows of their shoes. Then, a tiny sheet of paper slipped through the crack under the door. Whoever was there was now walking away. I heard their footsteps walking down the stairs.

I grabbed the folded up piece of paper.

'Knock 3 times on the floor if you want to meet.'

The next morning, the couple left early, or so I heard. I learned they were from Saugerties, and were co-owners of a jewelry line. When I thought about the kooky one's

(I wish I remembered their names, I just don't) urge to connect, I understood the feeling. I wondered if he was a mirror-image of myself at times. That wasn't the most curious part about him though. A few days after my stay, Holly told me that he left a review online. He completely ripped the hotel apart. He said that he got no sleep at all the one night he was there. He said that he wasn't able to sleep because he believed the hotel was haunted. The sound of footsteps kept him up all night; the sound of someone walking up and down a staircase.

OCTOBER 2020 PART II

October 4

When I used to think of love or what I wanted from it, it was not gentle. It definitely was not what I know now: kindness that can feel bittersweet. There's a silliness between Matthew and me that I hadn't experienced with someone before. It's childlike, recurring, and creative. Last night, at midnight, Matthew and I went into our building's hallway, and he filmed my impression of Shelley Duvall in *The Shining*. I ran down the hall in a black wig, in a bathrobe, holding a knife and flailed as much as I humanly could. My feet were inverted and dragging, wrists flying, the knife in my hand barely gripped. Shelley, to me, provides the best flail on film.

October 5

I bought a photo album a few weeks ago that can hold up to 600 pictures. It's larger than the average album, and is kitschy, even tacky looking, which is why I bought it. It's bright silver, with a faux-snake skin texture. If Andy Warhol's Factory were shrunk to size, it would be that album. I needed a place to put about 200 family pictures; the ones my dad gave me when I went to Florida in August. At first, I didn't know if these pictures still existed and if they did, did he have them?

The next few paragraphs are about to sound very procedural, and one of the first responses I had when I obtained these pictures was that I now have evidence of my actual family history. I had the photographs that proved my family was once a Brown-skinned, mixed-race family in Jamaica, living in Manchester Parish, Clarendon, and Kingston. I'd been researching for over two years. In 2017, I bought an AncestryDNA kit, partially because I remembered all of the rumors when I was growing up. I always heard whispers about my family's history, and that they were part Black. In retrospect, why wouldn't we be mixed-race? My family's name is Hopwood, and according to record, they lived in Jamaica for at least a century.

The rumors began when I was young, and they started with my sister's hair. My sister, Shea, had thick brown hair that was cut very short in her youth. This was in the mid '70s, and it was Shea's mother (Shea and I share the same father), who insisted her hair be cut short.

Because of Shea's curls and texture, her hair at a short length resembled an afro. By the time Shea was living with our father and her stepmom (Carrie, my mom), she was allowed to grow her hair however she liked. My mom told me that Shea would ride her bike home from school and run to the bathroom as soon as she got in, ready to brush and blow-dry her hair in an attempt to flatten and straighten it as best she could. When Shea was 20 years old, Carrie brought her to her hair salon (among one of Carrie's many hobbies, one was owning a hair salon named 'Septembers,' yes with 's' at the end). The salon wasn't open that day, so they had the place to themselves. Carrie washed, brushed, and took a pick to Shea's hair. For what exact reason, I don't know. There are polaroids of Shea, sitting in an empty salon, her hair in its natural state: full of curls, volume, and layers. Her dark roots in the center provided a strong contrast to the bleach-blonde on top.

Throughout elementary, middle, and high school, I was told that I was part Native American, our lineage coming from the Creek and Cherokee tribes. The funny thing is, it seems that almost all white Americans have a bit of 'Cherokee' in them. If they take a DNA test, they may find out otherwise. As a kid, I tanned quickly, was always asked if I'd been to the beach or tanning salon (which I found humorous) and was consistently mistaken for being Italian, sometimes Greek, or Jewish, and even Puerto Rican.

When I was seventeen, we had to present an extensive family tree for a class project. My dad drove me to his mother's, where she showed me the same pictures that my father gave to me last month. There was this one picture that I always remembered vividly. It was a family portrait of my great-great-grandparents, and their three sons, which included Alexander, my great-grandfather. The three boys were all very close in age, and stared somewhat blankly into the camera. I pictured them being fidgety, even though they appeared quite stoic for such young boys. Their mother stood above them. She looked, what you could describe as average. Her hair was pinned in an updo, her lips thin, her eyes looked a bit intense but were unremarkable in a way. Her features could be described as sharp.

Her husband sat to her left and wore a confident smile. It's striking because people generally did not smile in photographs at the turn of the century. This man, my great-great-grandfather was undeniably Black. His complexion was dark, his nose prominent and wide, his hair trimmed as short as could be. His lips were not thin like his wife's, but were full. The picture was in black and white, so it's hard to tell but his eyes looked light, which suggested a partial European background. At the bottom of the photograph, in a hand-written note, it read *Joseph Hopwood– Plantation Owner.*

When I ordered my AncestryDNA kit, I found the process to be very simple. For $99, you spit in a vial, mail it to a

I could hardly see
find
kill.
It felt like the polite thing to do.

lab, and in a few weeks results will tell you where your family originates from. As expected, my results varied; I was English, Scottish, African (specifically from Ghana and the Ivory Coast regions), Welsh and Irish. Native American, obviously, was not on the list.

As a teenager, when I was rifling through photographs with my grandmother, she never said 'My family was Black'. There was no acknowledgment that when we came across a picture of herself as a little girl in Kingston, she could have easily been considered a 'colored girl' at the time. I remember seeing a picture of her mother (who was also born in Jamaica and of mixed race) when she was about sixteen, and she wore her hair in two braids. My grandmother explained that she was paying homage to her roots, since her background was 'Native American'. Looking at the pictures, back then, I recognized that there was an otherness to my family members. I had not yet known what it was 'to pass'. I simply saw that there was something different between the people in those photographs and what I thought of as an average white person.

After my DNA results came through, that's when I really dove into my research. I began to build a family tree and I found photographs of aunts, uncles, cousins in Jamaica by sorting through other people's family trees online, who were a proven DNA match. Then I dove in, deep-dive style. I found my family's name on message boards dating back to 2007. Someone wrote that the Hopwood's family secrets were the 'worst kept secrets' in what I assume was the white upper class in Kingston, Jamaica. I found the wife of my great-uncle, who lived in Minnesota. She told me that when her husband (my grandmother's brother) was a child, school children threw rocks at him and called him 'Chocolate.' I found NYC immigration logs, naturalization papers, census reports dating back to the turn of the century. I saw that my family was listed as Black and living in a Harlem apartment in 1920. By 1950, everyone was listed as white and living in a family-owned home in Queens.

When my dad handed me the boxes with family photographs nearly spilling out of them, once belonging to my grandmother, I saw another story. I saw a story of Jamaican immigrants, a story of pre-WWII New York City. And I saw an album, a cataloging of my grandmother's life from being a young girl to being a young mother. The deeper I went into the pile, the older the photographs became, and the complexions of those photographed became darker as the years receded. I wasn't the only one taking notice.

'Look at your grandmother here. Look how dark she was. I'm telling you, it's like they were chameleons,' my dad said.

The analogy was fitting to say the least. Finally, I found the picture I had been looking for. The picture of my great-great- grandparents, with the inscription, *Joseph Hopwood–Plantation Owner.*

'See what it says there. Plantation owner,' my dad said.

'And you see that he is Black,' I replied.

My father and I had only briefly discussed race in our family. I think for a while, I used a bit of a filter with him because I was cautious or maybe cowardly of what I could say and what his limitations were as far as discussion. My dad, whose name is John, or 'Johnny' as his bar friends call him, reminds me of a real-life Harvey Keitel. He's from New York City and has a quiet but distinctly strong energy to him. He communicates more with glances and nods than he does with words. A part of 1950s New York will always be with him. Two years ago, he came for a brief visit and met Matthew for the first time. I swear he said something about taking him out or breaking his legs if anything happened to me. It was something very cliché and hetero, but I think he meant it. When we sat down to eat at an Italian restaurant in Brooklyn, he took a look around, surveying his surroundings.

'This reminds me of the bar in *A Bronx Tale*, you know with all the bikers. 'Now youse can't leave.' Good movie,' he said.

And like many men who grew up in the city during the fifties, he's seen a lot, and experienced more by the age of ten than some have by the age of forty. Among those things learned and experienced was racism and as a white man, he has shown what he learned. When I was young, I would let him know that I didn't like or approve when he would look at his neighbors in South Florida and make a comment about the 'browning of America' when he saw a Black person tending to their front lawn. It didn't matter though, he didn't seem to hear me. A couple of years ago, when I was doing most of our family research, I asked him what he thought or knew about his mother's side of the family being Black. I was nervous, and I thought he was going to shut me down.

'Well, you know, I think of it like, uh... I think of it like a milkshake. It's like a vanilla shake and you got a chocolate swirl in there,' he said.

The strange thing was, I was both disappointed and assuaged by his answer. It's an awful analogy that reduces, well, everything, but it was an acknowledgement. Now I sit here with him, looking at his Black ancestors. When there's photographic evidence, and there are two eyes looking at the same picture, it opens a discussion because there is a visual experience being shared.

'Can I give you my theory?' I asked.

I continued, 'So, I think the Hopwoods owned a plantation and owned slaves. The sons that were had with the women who were enslaved, well, I don't know if it worked out like how it would have worked out in America. Usually, those children would be sold. I think maybe the sons were raised, or stolen, by the plantation owners and given the family name. Then, the plantation was given to them and they took over as the owners... but I don't know, that's one possibility. There seems like there may have been a lot of possibilities...'

'I think you're right,' he said.

I was surprised when he said that because it showed that he was letting me take the lead. He was allowing me to reframe the past.

When I think about the picture of my dad's uncle and his uncle's cousin, arms around each other, smiling, on a front porch in 1930s New York and the fact that one is white and the other is a handsome boy with brown skin, both in oversized suits — I think, how was this not discussed? He told me it was never talked about, as if there was nothing to be said. And again, I just think, how? Or perhaps, how much was said in whispers that he could not hear? How do hushed tones and lies affect the eyes that are unsure of what they see?

This past summer, I wanted to learn more, maybe find a way of reaching those from the past. I took pictures of my ancestors and laid them out on my bed. Then, I printed a short story of mine, named 'Seven.' I cut up passages of 'Seven,' and threw the pieces of text in a pile. As I did this, I thought of my ancestors. What could they have not said then that they could say now? Would they like a chance to speak?

At random, I laid the cut up pieces of text over their portraits. This is what a few of them read:

'The mirror didn't offend him.'
'A group of men touched me first.'
'Took a hanger, it ended well.'
'I love you, with fervor.'

One of my great-grandfather's cousins was named Alwyn Hopwood, the youngest amongst a dozen or so children. Alwyn resembled a doe, his eyes were wide and unassuming, his hair the color of wheat. He was one of the only relatives that I found who had little to no history attached to his name. He was born in 1908, and died in 1934, at only 26 years old. I don't know how he died, as I could not find a death certificate. I don't know if he ever married, or if he had children.

Alwyn, crystallized in his youth, was a mystery. I wanted to find a way for him to be seen and to be in the present. Last July, while visiting Leo upstate, I took Alwyn's picture to a tattoo artist and painter who specialized in portraits. On my upper right arm, Alwyn now sits. Above his head, and across his chest, are words from *The Comet*, a short story by W.E.B. Du Bois. They read, 'A thought divine, splendid'.

October 7, 4:45 am

Is it because of October, because it's a witchy time, that I'm up at this hour? Is it because I have a lot to say in a not-so-sequential order? Is it muscle memory flexing itself, as I would normally be up at this time if I were drunk? Is it because I'm thinking about how I was *officially* let go from my job at Homecoming yesterday? I can't speak for someone else, but I can speak for myself, when I say that it feels like there's something ending for me. I no longer have a professional job or title to live by, or a workplace to return to. My time with Homecoming Hotel has an official beginning and end: 2016–2020.

I realized that my time there has been the same amount of time that Trump has been in office. Wednesday, November 9, 2016 was my third day at Homecoming, and the first day after the election. I remember guests checking out, with somber faces, and saying 'I'm sorry' to reception. I saw a bro-dude that morning, near 8th Avenue, who I'm guessing worked in finance, and may have been wearing a sweater vest (they love those). He was talking loudly into his phone and with excitement said, 'We won! He got in! He got in!' What I saw was someone who thought they were going to get rich, or richer. All the other stuff about Trump that he may or may not have liked didn't matter. He saw him as a success, a symbol of fortune. This guy was Gordon Gecko in 2016, or was a Gordon Gecko, Jr. It's crazy to me how much of the movie *Wall Street* and 1980s excess can still be seen today. It all just seems so fucking dated, yet some people my age, who were of the graduating classes in the early 2000s, they are second generation Gordon Geckos. And they helped push Trump into office.

I wondered if the Gordon Gecko guy could be a guest of the hotel, the kind of guest who wanted to be seen amongst artist types but tossed around the word 'fag' when laughing with his buddies. That's what the clientele of Homecoming eventually became: bros and techies willing to pay good money to feel trendy. That said, Homecoming Hotel was an era in NYC. But also, let's not forget, while Homecoming brought money into what was described as a fledgling or 'need-of-attention' neighborhood, they bought out New Yorkers, turning their homes into hotel rooms for profit. Its history is not an easy or clean one. It's like a kaleidoscope in a way, and what you see depends on what angle you're peering through. If you look through the lens of those who were pushed out, you must pause and think of their loss. What does the popularity of a place matter if it means taking the home of another?

Homecoming's 'golden era,' post tenant eviction, you could say, was when they first opened ten years ago. I heard stories of what it was like in the beginning. A non-stop party. There's this myth that Homecoming was full of misfits, many of them Queer artists, who came together under the focused and kind eye of its founder, a West Coast real estate developer with a fondness for late nights, drugs, and disco. Barely anyone who worked there had hospitality experience, but they came together, and took this crazy idea made of love, art, and commerce, and formed a hotel. And they made it work. There was parties, and cocaine, and fucking, and heart, and a belief filled with good intentions that kept the hotel operations turning, one hungover shift at a time.

I don't doubt that some of this is true. By the time my time was wrapping up at Homecoming, the hotel became sterile. Like all things past their prime, imitation sneaks its way in: even middle management couldn't camouflage their corporate suits by way of Converse shoes and acid-washed denim. Those calling the shots were no longer interested in art or community (even if it all began as a product of gentrification). Still, I ask, how initially invested were they? Did their greed always come first or was it dormant, sitting side-by-side with their good intentions, then washed over them like they were sand castles during a high-tide?

I keep thinking about a joke made by the General Manager, the one who told me I was spoon fed shit (who incidentally was the replacement of the previous GM; a born again Christian who racked up at least three sexual misconduct accusations). It wasn't so much a joke as it was a comment. Someone in our lead staff morning meeting mentioned that one of the tenants in the building (who did not accept the buy out when ownership took the property over) was sitting outside of the entrance, with his music blasting through his headphones. I assume this may have been mentioned because, maybe, the tenant was seen as an eyesore since he was a 70-year-old man with a limp who tended to not pay much mind to the trendy hotel guests strolling by.

Addressing the staff as his audience, the GM said, 'Those pots that he sits on have huge spikes around the edge. Maybe he'll sit on one and bleed out and we'll get to use his room.'

I didn't find the comment funny, not only because it was grotesque, but there wasn't actually anything witty or humorous in its context. What struck me the most though, was not the comment itself (I was used to the cryptic tone of the GM) but the fact that everyone laughed. Whether they actually thought that comment was funny or not, I do not know; but they laughed, holding their binders or papers, snickering as they trickled down the hall. There was one person besides myself that didn't laugh, or snicker, or giggle. Knowing them as I did, I assume it's because they didn't feel the need to demonstrate obedience over showing decency in regards to human life.

The other truth to Homecoming Hotel is that some of my greatest friends came from that place. I felt a closeness and bond, and still do, to many people there and since they've closed down, I think about some of them almost daily. I follow them on social media and I care about what they're doing, or listening to, or going through, or marrying, or who they're breaking up with, if someone's mom or dad is okay. I can say that I wanted to be there at Homecoming because of the mythos I thought it was. Something made from nothing, something flawed, threaded with art, creativity and mistakes. A group of people, not a corporation, who honestly cared for one another.

October 10

The forward to John Rechy's *Sexual Outlaw* reads that he wanted to make a 'prose documentary.' I suppose I feel the same. I took a look at what I've written and compared it to my writing from seven years ago. I was recording a diary then, as I am now. I didn't have as much to say seven years ago, though I think I felt just as much, if not more. I wonder if it is a coincidence that I'm recording between the months of August to November, in 2020, just as I did in 2013. Seven years ago, I thought a bottle of wine was going to make my writing better, deeper, more truthful, or effective. My recordings were darker, stranger. I made real-life characters into vampires, vampires who engaged in incest. I don't know, I had only been in therapy for six months, and maybe that was my way of using metaphor. It also showcased my love for the Undead.

Back then, at thirty, I cared less about recording what was actually happening in real-time (which I still did plenty of) and cared more about putting on a show of what was going through my head. I compare it to being a streaker on live television. I wanted to be nude in front of an audience, to make it impossible for them to look away. Then, after my performance, I'd run offstage where no one would find me. I don't think of recording in the same way anymore. It's not just for show, it's for the truth and it must remain, even if I run away.

My voice and experiences, how I relate those experiences to others, may continue to change as time goes on. But as I write now, right now, this is first-person-present truth. I look at gay literature, portrayals of gay life that have gained reputations as 'classics.' Andrew Holleran's *Dancer from the Dance*, a novel known for being one of the first, honest portrayals of gay (male) metropolitan life in the 1970s. I couldn't wait for that book to end, partially because I couldn't stand how Anthony Mallone was written: a good-looking NYC transplant, with a murky, closeted past, who fell into the club scene, drowned in his desires, and trapped himself in a life of vapidness where there was no escape. I mean, to be fair, that might be 20% of NYC gays at this very moment. Point is, I didn't relate, and I didn't feel that it gave me anything to hang onto.

John Rechy though, he's another story. The author of *City of Night*, and *Sexual Outlaw*, took his experiences as both a writer and a hustler and gave the reader the meat they needed to cut through. *City of Night* was a classic, and *Sexual Outlaw* was an experiment, and Rechy's later works were pulp-trash, but he gave us something that other Queer novels did not: first-person realism. A recording of events from one's life and the people who enter it, replacing romanticism with grit.

Seven years ago, when I'd write about myself, I made myself into a Lolita, vampiric character. Is that because forbidden intimacy can feel the most intimate? I wrote about seducing cis-hetero men as if it were a sort of power, to be able to turn. When really, couldn't anyone possess that power, especially if the other is looking to explore, to try something new? I may just be looking at it now from more of an analytical or realistic point of view. I missed out on having male friendships as a teen, and what it was to be naked, to discover with someone for their first time; two boys and their youth pressed against each other, fumbling and uncertain. In retrospect, I bet most gays didn't have that experience as it sounds like something from the twink section of a porn site. With that said, I never looked at being with a straight man as a means to fatten my ego. In a way, it was like I was helping them (despite their possible internalized homophobia) and I saw power in that. There is also a bit of magick in that: to disarm, embolden, to wrap around, to please, to release. It resembles a vampire, some might say.

October 11

One of the only goals that I have at the moment is to create every day, to write and record. I can do so, having the luxury of comfort being here and living with Matthew. He makes our home a funhouse and fills it with nostalgia. Our living room is decorated with ghost decorations hanging from the ceiling. When we watch horror films at night, images of old-time, cartoonish ghosts fly across the walls from a Halloween-theme projector. He has toys and gadgets for every season, holiday, and celebration.

There are a pair of wooden, sliding doors that separate our living room from the rest of the apartment. At night, when we're watching *The Haunting of Bly Manor*, I close the doors, turn off the lights, and switch on Matthew's ghost projector. I'm able to fantasize here, and I get to be the moody, quasi-creepy child that I've always been. And right now, being unemployed, I don't have to think about work, if someone is calling out, if a guest is going to contact me while I'm off, if I'm missing an urgent email. I am fortunate enough to be in this current position and not worry about money. I'm lucky to even have the chance to feel gratitude, being in the position that I'm in.

I'm taking what has presented itself to me and unapologetically taking advantage of it: being financially stable, having a partner who is a nice, good man, and for once I'm not going to let time be my enemy. At this moment, time is all I have.

And with time and leisure, I hope to add a bit of travel, which may bring pleasure. This morning, I asked Matthew if he wanted to spend some time upstate once his freelance, stay-at-home, contract job is finished on Friday. It's the perfect season to visit north of the city, and we could make a pit stop and visit Tarrytown, home of Sleepy Hollow, home of the Headless Horseman. I also want us to meet Rodrigo. Rodrigo and I have chatted through Instagram for a couple months now (the older daddy-type that lives in Woodstock, who said he wanted Matthew to watch us play together). He's in his early fifties, and as an older man, there is a deep set handsomeness in his features. Usually, if someone remains that handsome at that age, if you see a picture of them in their twenties, their beauty was almost uncomfortable; too pretty, too youthful, too symmetrical.

Rodrigo owns a house in Woodstock, the area Matthew and I tend to visit. He said he'd like to meet Matthew and myself the next time we're there. At his request, he'd like for the three of us to spend ample time sucking each other off. Also, Rodrigo has a thing for feet, a desire that I do not share. This morning, I snuck into the bathroom and trimmed two of my toenails after he requested a foot pic.

'They're so nice,' he said.

He probably didn't notice that I was strategically hiding a small bunion.

But what Rodrigo really wants, and what I also want badly, is for him to cum inside me while Matthew watches. There's a bit of power play in this scene, but who said that power and pleasure shouldn't mix? To give in to someone, their brazen act, myself and my partner as witness, to feel both its high and comedown; it's one of the most intimate scenes three people can share.

October 12, 8:00 am

At some point, after primarily being indoors for seven months, currently waiting on my severance check from the hotel to arrive, I have to start trusting and relying on my intuition in regards to the future and what to do next. Being inside for so long, I wonder, will the outside world and its energy be welcoming to me? Is it a dead energy out there or is it so chaotic that it needs to spend more time sorting itself? For now, what I can do is to continue creating from what I have within, both within myself and within my apartment. I can learn, I can research, and gain knowledge from books and film. I can provide myself an education. That's what I've been doing thus far, and will continue to do so.

It's raining all day today, an afterthought of one of the few hurricanes that have struck the Gulf Coast this season. To my left are my family photos, sitting in their frames, ready to be hung. I haven't put them up yet for a couple reasons. I'm not looking forward to measuring and hammering, for one. I've also been hesitant because a part of me feels as though I'm raising the dead. *Do they want to be on display and exist in the world again?*

1:33 pm

I decided to mount the photographs, as a collage, and in the center are two sisters, aunts Violet and Hazel, sitting on the front porch steps of a house in Jamaica. Below them is a picture of mid-century New York City. To their left, is a picture of John and Stafford, Jr., two cousins in 1930s New York. One is white and the other is Brown, both wearing suits that you would never find a teenager wearing today. They're both smiling, looking boyishly happy.

This didn't feel like I was awakening the dead. It felt like a realization, a realization that everyone pictured were living beings with their own force that was uniquely theirs.

October 13

I've been lost in fantasy since I woke up. I chatted online with someone yesterday who lives just down the street, on 4th Avenue. He told me he wanted to meet up and suck my cock, and I'm open to the invitation. To be honest, he reminds me of me ten years ago. Same facial structure, hair style, skin tone. I don't know his name, not yet. I picture us naked, making out, jerking each other off. I want to do more than just have him suck my dick. I want him naked, sucking me off, sucking Matthew off, and I'd like him to think about it while he goes about his day. I want him as our boy; we can fuck each other, lie on our couch, be awkward, squirm a bit, watch TV. Our cum will become what is familiar to him.

This morning, this desire, it was too strong. I asked Matthew if he wanted to jerk off, and we did and came together. It's almost 11 am now, and it was pleasurable, but I want more. I also know how fast and hard I fall into fantasy. I don't even know this kid's name and yet I want him as much as I do. I won't deny my desire as I already have a long enough history of doing so. I have to remember, though, that when my fantasies are brought into reality, they become something else.

In February, before lockdown, I went to meet someone that I had been chatting with via Squirt. He lived in Bay Ridge, which was close to where we are. He was a little older, and I think he was originally from Russia. I had a vision of an older man, distinguished, maybe a little worn. I thought of this person as someone I could bring pleasure to, for him to be at ease when we meet. I'd get to experience being with someone who was just a little tired, hopeful, virile.

On the train ride to his place, my thoughts took a different turn. I had an inclination that it was unknown what I was in for, that this visit could go a few different ways. When I arrived at his building, it felt like it had been abandoned. The foyer was empty, and actually had a breeze running through it. The tile was old, very old, and had a film of dirt over the surface. Scraps of trash littered throughout even looked lonely and neglected. He lived on the fourth floor, and I started to climb the drab marble staircase. I looked at the directions he texted me, and found his door. I asked myself, does it really matter what his building looks like? I've lived in buildings like this, and I wouldn't want someone judging me. Gently, I knocked on his door and immediately it cracked open, and was left slightly ajar. I walked in and saw him standing there, in his living room. He was wearing old flannel pajama pants and a loose-fitting tank top. He looked older than in his pictures. His body was not as fit as presented, but I've never cared what someone's body is like.

'Hi, hello, come in,' he said.

I slowly entered. The apartment was a one bedroom and obviously, he had not prepared for my arrival. It's not that there was clutter, if anything, the apartment looked sparse. It reminded me of the lobby; a little sad and in need of Windex and a paper towel.

'You can take your shoes off there, and hang your coat if you want,' he said.

I slipped off my shoes, and hung my coat on a crowded coat rack. It felt like I was getting rid of my security, appearing like I had every intention of staying a while. I wasn't sure what I was feeling, honestly. I was pushing down my automatic responses.

'Do you smoke?' he asked. He was walking through his kitchen.

'Uh, yeah, I mean, sometimes, yeah,' I said.

He took that as a yes and started packing weed into a one-hitter. I sat down on the couch. He came over, holding his one-hitter, and sat beside me. He asked if I watched Netflix, and I said that I do. I'm not sure if he even named a specific show on Netflix or not. The conversation was hard to get through, and his accent was much thicker than I anticipated. This is when I started reasoning with myself. Jerking off with him on the couch would be fine with me. Once his dick was out, then I might start to get turned on. I took a hit, and repeated this thought to myself.

'What would you like to do?' he asked.

He was grinning, and he did have a cute, crooked smile.

'We could start by jacking off.'

'Let's go in there,' he said. He motioned his head to the bedroom.

I followed him and inside the room, it was dark, the shades pulled all the way down. Everything here feels empty. He starts to take off his clothes, and I do the same.

I looked down. He was already getting hard. His dick was pale with a pink head and looked heavy. It was thick and round, and resembled a sausage. We reached out our hands and started pulling on one another. His shoulders were broad, his stance strong. He couldn't have been over 5'8', as I stood a few inches above him. His touch and his squeeze were getting more intense.

'Do you suck?' he asked.

I stood there, looking at him. I hadn't decided yet what I wanted to do.

'Maybe,' I replied.

He scoffed and smiled in response. This felt like a stand-off. I didn't feel unsafe, but there was a forcefulness to him, and I didn't exactly have the time and space to contemplate over it.

I bent down and put his cock in my mouth. Immediately, he took my head and started shoving it back and forth, back and forth. I didn't like the way his skin tasted. It tasted like he didn't shower or bathe that day. I could taste the day before on him. We moved to the bed. I laid adjacent to the headboard, and sprawled my legs open. He began to suck ravenously. Of course, there was a harshness to his suck and I thought: this is his primary physical contact. I don't know if he's ever applied softness to a random encounter, but he sure didn't act like it. He flipped me over and started eating my ass. His tongue was so deep, his stubble rubbed against me, almost burning, but not in a bad way. He sat me up on my knees, wrapped his arm over me, and pressed his cock against me. I realized he's getting me ready to fuck, but this is not going to happen.

I turned around, facing him, and started jerking him off again. We fall horizontally on the bed, him on top of me. He's stroking me too. His broad, heavy shoulders are against mine, in this dark room, and we jerked each other off faster and faster. We wrapped our arms around each other's backs, and he buried his head into my shoulder.

'I'm going to cum,' he said.

'Me too.'

We held each other as we came on our stomachs. I had a dreamy moment of calm. We're all just looking for someone to feel close to, even if it's for a few moments. I looked around his room. His walls were bare except for a framed picture of a saint on the wall. Maybe he was religious. I remember he said he was a hairdresser. I tried to imagine what his salon looked like. I thought I could see his lonely life when he was in Russia, where he wasn't yet out. I didn't actually know anything about his life, my fantasy was getting ahead of me. But I felt empathy for him in that moment, in that room, while we dressed.

On the train ride home, I was in a daze. I was not in any sense of the word, 'present.' It really felt as if I was in a portal of some kind. I thought of all the men, in the past, who had to hide who they were. I thought of how just obtaining moments of closeness with another man, fleeting moments, were enough, just for those few short minutes. But it wasn't enough to live that way: to live like you were underground, to constantly be hunting for just a few moments of closeness and pleasure to share with another, to do this for a lifetime.

When I walked into our apartment, I saw the wall that Matthew created. It's a wall of artwork, made by our friends, most of whom are artists. They drew portraits of us, sometimes of just our faces, in some cases, our bodies, too. Many of these paintings, drawings, and illustrations were given to us as wedding presents. I looked up at the wall, and saw Matthew and me, and burst into tears.

October 14

This morning at about 10 am, I was getting out of the shower when I heard my phone ring. The screen read 'Mom Home.' I knew what this call was going to be about. Last night, she called me and said she's been restless as she waits for the results of her biopsy. Her doctor had called her yesterday, but she wasn't able to get to her phone. He left a voicemail that said, 'I have your test results and we'll be in touch this week,' which to be fair, sounds very standard. She went to call him back but he had already left for the day.

'I just want to know if it's cancerous or not,' she told me.

As my phone rang, I grabbed the towel hanging from the bathroom door, wiping my hands.

'Hello?'

'Hi, Jay.'

There was a pause.

'I got the test results back,' she said.

'Okay.'

'And... they came back... as...'

She takes a long pause, longer than the first.

'Benign.'

I'm relieved. I could have done without the Ed McMahon announcing the winner on *Star Search* approach, but nonetheless, I am both relieved and happy for her. I hope she spends the rest of her day doing whatever she likes; riding her bike; smoking an e-cigarette while watching hours of CNN commentary; or reading a New Age book while drinking celery juice. Whatever fits her fancy, I hope she enjoys her day.

October 15

Twelve years ago, in my first New York apartment, I was in my bedroom and my roommate, Angelica, was in the living room, right outside my door. To say that Angelica was inquisitive is an understatement. She's almost morbidly interested in what lies beneath. I got this impression that what was beneath my skin was for her to play with.

She called out from the next room. 'Are you a virgin?'

I would have done anything to avoid that question. I was 25 years old, not yet out, and yes, I was a virgin. To this day, I'm not sure how I managed to avoid questions about sex as much as I did.

'Um... no,' I answered.

'Oh, okay. You don't ever talk about sex, so I wasn't sure,' she said.

This is when I'd give a rehearsed reply. 'I don't mean to not talk about it, I don't know, it's not something that I consciously don't talk about.'

I knew that Angelica wasn't satisfied with that answer and who would be? I also knew I was giving her ammo or a charge to study me and find out more. Moments like this, when I was asked about sex, it's like I would temporarily black out. My body felt a response of fear and panic, then I would deflect as best as I could.

Angelica's prying irritated me, but it could have been necessary during that time; to have someone push me just a little bit more than they should. She took a lot of pictures of me back then. She was always playing around with film and cameras. She objectified me, made me feel like a subject, but again, maybe that was something I needed. To know that there was interest in who I was, to know that there was interest in what I withheld.

October 16

In 2005 or 2006, I started to write down my thoughts, or notes, or whatever it was that I was contemplating. I've tried to find a certain notebook, hoping that it didn't get discarded during the move to New York. I remember one of the notes I had written asked, 'What is my relationship with men?' I was taking the beginning steps to coming out, but that question remains as relevant today as it did then.

A Phantom Craving

Today, for the whole day, I've been feeling this gnawing need to be naked, and hard, and making out with someone, someone new perhaps. Yes, Matthew is in the next room, but I'm not going to interrupt him as he works. Besides, it's the exploration of something new at this time that I am craving so badly. I could invite the young guy down the street over. I told him that while he gives Matthew and me head, he must be naked. I'm sure he won't have a problem abiding by the request. I'm not going to invite him over, though.

Next week, Matthew and I are driving to Woodstock. Matthew found out that his art will be featured in a barn-style Queer art exhibit. I'm glad he's getting showcased. The art world is incestuous in the city, with an overemphasis on what is defined as fine art. Sometimes I think Matthew questions if he's included in that world, despite the obvious talent that he has. For him to receive recognition is something always welcomed and deserved. We're going up for two nights, and we're going to meet Rodrigo while we're there. That's why I'm not going to meet the 4th Ave. neighborhood kid a week before and possibly expose everyone. There's an uptick in Covid cases in Brooklyn right now, and I just don't need the added worry or what-ifs. Rodrigo and I messaged each other about how exactly 'quarantined' we've been. He hasn't seen many people, and said he has one regular fuck buddy in Woodstock. If anything, just having the discussion put me at ease.

It's also been one of the most dreary days that I can remember. There's been a light ongoing rain for almost twelve hours now. I took a nap, but not for long. For hours, I've been edging on and off in bed, and I'm almost too good at it at this point. Maybe it's quarantine, maybe it's the new moon, but it doesn't seem like I'm the only person feeling this way. I came across a cute guy named Joey on Instagram, who lives in Texas, and sent a heart-eyes emoji to him in response to a picture of him in a robe, holding a cup of coffee. Within minutes we were sending videos of each other fucking, and not even using the time limit photo bomb option, either.

October 18

This morning, I logged onto Squirt and was messaging with someone named 'BKGuy.' He claimed to be bi and a New York native and said that he knew where all the good, truly underground cruising spots were, not those 'gross video stores.' It was like he wanted to give information. He told me about a man on 19th Street, between 3rd and 4th Avenue, who worked in a wood shop. He said he was good looking, with dirty blond hair and a hot cock. He said the wood shop had a black, unmarked door. It looked like a warehouse, but was some sort of workshop for furniture or sets or something. He said that yesterday he had been there himself. He told me that he had heard from someone about this place, and the guy that works there. He wrote that he went inside, pretended to not know where he was, as if he took a wrong turn, and then asked to use the bathroom. Once inside, he cracked the door, just ajar, and began stroking. A few minutes later, the guy manning the wood shop stepped in. The two of them stroked each other, gave each other head and then came.

BKGuy wrote that if I go down there, to text him, he'd wander into the shop and join. The thought of it excited me, and I wondered if I'd actually go. I've avoided meeting with anyone from the site during the pandemic, because it feels like too much of a risk. I took a bath, I stretched, I put on my running clothes. I'd run down to 19th Street, just to look, I told myself. I just want to see if the black door is there. I didn't say anything to Matthew, not yet, because I wasn't sure if I'd go inside.

I began to run, listening to music, loud industrial music, and the street numbers started becoming smaller. 40th Street, 35th Street, 25th Street. Soon, I was near 21st, 20th, and then 19th. I rounded the corner and looked for the address, building number 132. I passed by a black, unmarked door with the number 132 written above it. I kept walking. I don't think I'm going to go in. Sometimes, I just like to see, to know, or to wonder. I walked up to 4th Avenue, then turned down 19th Street again, on the opposite side of the street. I was getting closer to 132. I crossed the street, the door was right there. It's probably locked. I went up to the door and turned the knob, and it swung open.

Inside, it looked like a construction site. There was wood and machines, and saws everywhere. I heard a robotic voice say, 'Front Door Open.' Around the corner walked over a man, very good looking, butch, with a friendly smile. He might have been wiping his hands. He looked like what an actor portraying a man in a wood shop would look like. His hair was brown, not blond. I remember the BKGuy said, if a man with dark hair is there, just say you got the wrong address and walk out.

'Hey,' he said.

'Hi... was this ever a bike shop?' I asked.

'No, no, it's a workshop for set production.' He was smiling.

'Oh, alright, I must have the wrong place,' I said.

I started to walk out, and he began to turn the other way. His head was ever so slightly turned to the side, his eyes somewhere near the ground, as if he wasn't looking at the floor, but to his left, towards me. I turned around and walked out. I messaged BKGuy, 'Not today, the dark-haired guy was there.' He messaged back, 'Did he have a beard and blackish hair?' 'No,' I texted. I knew then, that was him, that was the guy. The demeanor, the friendliness, the cocking of the head. BKGuy said, 'I should have told you the dark-haired guy has a beard. Sorry, man. You can go back and ask where the bike shop is. Easy fix.' I messaged back, 'No, I like to get things right the first time.'

I started jogging home, and it felt like I lost something. My heart was beating, and I felt frantic. Like I let something go, when I shouldn't have. I ran back to 19th Street and I walked past the black door again, but I didn't go in.

I couldn't make myself go back in. I walked past the door and began to run home. I ran so fast, passing maybe even scaring people next to me on the sidewalk. I felt angry, and sad, and like I failed at something, that I missed an opportunity. I ran faster. 'Go home,' I was whispering, muffled underneath my mask.

'Go home, go home, go home.'

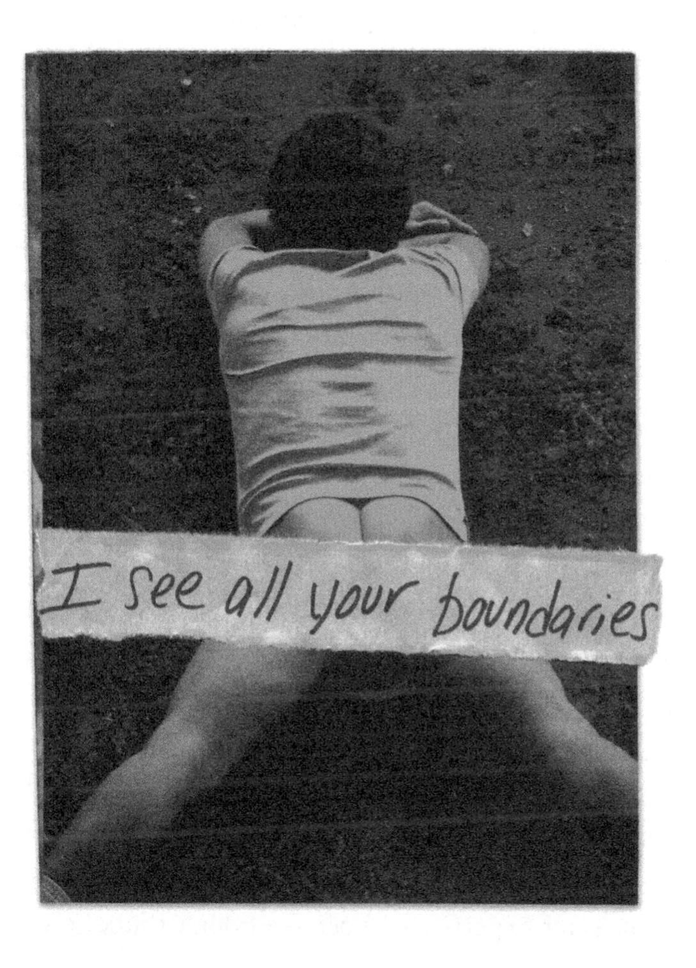

October 19

Yesterday, I got a text from Leo that said:

'I know this is out of the blue. I've been giving a lot of thought about conflicting emotions that I've had for a long time. I love you so much, but for now on, I can't be involved with anyone in open relationships. I'll always be there for you if you need anything.'

The first thing I saw when I opened up my phone was, 'I love you so much,' and I wasn't sure what was going on. I read the full text once and immediately replied with, 'Hey, no worries at all, all that matters is that I have you as a friend.' I answered so quickly because I didn't want to spend too much time in that place where there are overlapping emotions, but those emotions are there anyways, whether you want to recognize them or not. I felt a little disappointed, and there's a feeling of resentment there, but that resentment is only taking up a small portion of what I feel.

I knew that Leo had a habit of sleeping with guys in open relationships. He said it was because they usually are more fearless in bed. This is in contrast to what he says is the 'vanilla' nature of single men who are looking to practice monogamy. I've known that Leo wants a partner, and I cannot argue against the security that comes with having one. I imagine that there is quite a bit that he has not experienced because I don't think he's had a steady partner, at least not outside of college. When he says something like, 'I wish I had someone I could creampie while he tells me that his ass is mine,' that's when I wonder how far he's gone with someone. Not to say that a long-term couple wouldn't say that to one another, but it feels like something you'd wish for as you fall in love, and not after the fact.

The part of me that does have some resentment is that I allowed there to be such freedom in our interactions. He could say or do whatever he liked. He has a rude streak, but for the most part, I'd let that go. I was very mindful of any emotional barriers he may have had, and I did not aim to cross them even if it crossed my mind. I allowed him to use his body and mine, in whatever way he pleased, be it impersonal, be it rough, be it coated with bits of humiliation. In many ways, I allowed him to lead in our friendship, though at times I thought I was silently steering the wheel. So, to have him say to me, with no lead up to this conversation, that we're done having a physical friendship, it feels like I don't get credit, like I was disruptive, when I felt that I was anything but.

Then, I take a step back. Maybe I was disruptive to him. If I never actually broached Leo's emotional landscape, then that means that I don't know much about it. I don't know what he didn't say in words, so I don't know if there were conflicting emotions about me, or if he ever had moments of feeling very strongly about me, moments that were heavier than friendship. He took a picture of me once, when we were on his couch and watching a movie. And I thought, is he capturing something that feels significant to him? There were moments when we'd lie in his bed, and I'd rest my head along his chest, always adorned with his gold crucifix, and it felt secure and sweet. I have to remember though, moments like that, are just moments for me. I have a husband and a life, only three hours away.

October 20

I'm mindful of the first thought that comes to me as I wake. I wonder if these thoughts are the result of a dream that I had throughout the night or if these are my purest thoughts and feelings, not yet filtered or interrupted by everyday life, social media, the news, even myself. Today, when I woke up, at a little past 5 am, I thought, I'm starving.

I'm starving for more sex, companionship, men, and exploration. Being married, for me, means that I found someone who will stand by my side and I by his. You cannot live though, just standing idly next to someone. I know it's a choice of how or where open relationships can go. Guy and Paul, the newly married couple who we jerked off on cam with, sent us pictures this morning of them hard in bed, their cocks rock hard and shadows from their bedroom blinds adding an artful touch that was probably intentional. Matthew and I sent pictures back, culminating in Matthew giving me head. I thoroughly enjoy feeling like I'm participating in communal sex, even if it's virtual. There's such safety there though, because it is online.

I'm hoping when we meet with Rodrigo in Woodstock this week, that some of the edginess I've been feeling as of late will be relieved. When we get back, maybe I'll talk to Matthew about the possibility of me joining Scruff or something similar again. I don't think I can deal with the closeted nature of Squirt anymore, although I've thought of that man in the wood shop, behind the black door, once a day. I remember how addicting hook-up apps could be. Searching, searching, always searching for something, anything. Wouldn't that be full circle? To go back to the site I met Matthew on six years ago. I have so much more now than I did then and I have shared so much with Matthew since then. Honestly, I doubt I'll go back to Scruff, or the apps, but I don't block the thought. To go back... to look and look and look... looking for what, exactly?

October 22

Matthew and I are in the same hotel we stayed in, near Woodstock, when we got married last year. Because of Covid and I'm assuming low occupancy, it feels like a ghostly inn, which of course, I like. The halls are dimmed and silent, the wait staff who work in the restaurant, or dining hall, loiter amongst themselves. We rented a car in Brooklyn and drove up this morning. We arrived before check-in, and decided to kill time, and go on a hike at a nearby trail.

Whenever we go on a hike, the same thing happens. Always, I walk in front of Matthew. My strides are longer, my steps broader than his. I am more likely than him to trip over branches or stones. Matthew walks behind me, and although it looks like I lead, he reminds me of which way to go or turn. I don't know if it's because I get lost in my thoughts while we're walking or maybe it feels like I'm following a path, though, I'm really just headed into the brush. I'm usually looking towards the ground, or only at the trees directly in front of me. I barely ever pay attention to the markers on the trees that are meant to guide. That is when Matthew says, 'This way.'

October 23

There's something nerve-wracking about the morning before you meet to have sex with someone new. I guess it also depends on the type of sex you'll be having, although that's not always the easiest thing to predict. I'm predicting that Rodrigo will be fucking me, so my food intake and what type of food I eat will have an affect. There's the age old question, to douche or not to douche? More often than not, I've had better experiences when I chose to not give myself an enema. I found that it loosens the gut too much. But gay men, I think, are often scared into the what-ifs. What if you don't Fleet and then things get messy and weird and complicated and you kill the scene and fuck up his bed? What if you're seen as lazy or dirty? These banal questions make the whole day leading up to potential sex feel rife with tension. Anxieties about the body and performance can fill your brain if you let them.

I have to ease into the day, to not think of anything too far ahead. Matthew and I are going to go on another hike, and then we have his art show after, and we'll meet at Rodrigo's around 8. It's hard for me to relax though, to get my mind at ease and my body to come down. As I woke up this morning, I thought, I've never had sex with someone in their fifties. There's a sense of dignity in the whole scenario; meeting a man, like Rodrigo, in a house that he owns, away from the city. I may write about these experiences and escapades very openly, but I also love the idea of be-

ing hidden, naked, fucking in a house in the woods, hours away from the city, away from friends, from strangers on the streets. It makes me feel less common, as if my desire is too strong for the dull concrete of the city, and instead, it must move as wildly as it wishes in the open terrain. Just as wild is how pretentious that sounds.

October 24

Before we left Rodrigo's last night, I excused myself to use the restroom. Inside, I jotted down a note in my phone. It read, 'We lay there.' There was a moment, longer than a moment, that I wanted to remember. Matthew, Rodrigo, and I were lying in Rodrigo's bed, we could hear the sound of crickets and insects from outside. We lay in silence, our eyes opening and closing. Matthew lay to my left, his head slightly turned, resting on my shoulder. I was in the middle of him and Rodrigo, and I recognized the peace that was in the room. Rodrigo lay to my right, his head on my chest, his arm wrapped around me. His body and his weight felt like it was content. Matthew and I have had threesomes before, but I never sought to lay there after, and bask with our third. In the past, I didn't wish to go there and I didn't feel, what you could say, was an affection for us as a unit. This time though, I let myself sink into the moment, being in the middle of these two, hearing the sound of crickets while the minutes passed on Rodrigo's digital alarm clock. Matthew and I would be leaving soon. It was already past midnight.

While I was nervous earlier in the day, before we met Rodrigo, my nerves started to dissipate on the car ride over to his place. This was probably because I was allowing myself to see humor in our situation. We had to drive for seven miles down a long, empty, nearly pitch-black road.

'Can you imagine if we're being catfished?' I said to Matthew.

'During spooky season, too...'

We made a left onto a dirt road, passing a large, red barn to our right. We drove on, eventually seeing Rodrigo's house, with decorative bulb lights strung along his porch. As we pulled up, I saw Rodrigo moving inside.

'We're here,' I texted.

When we stepped out of the car, our feet made scratchy noises on the rock and gravel-filled driveway. Rodrigo appeared, opening up his screen door. He was even better looking in real-life than he was online. He was maybe 5'9', broad-shouldered, sturdy, looked like he had strong arms and legs, had a white beard, thick, jet-black eyebrows and a head of gray hair. I realize I'm describing him as if he's an actual stallion, but in a way, he is. Rodrigo was casual in his approach as we entered, offering me a seltzer, and Matthew a glass of red wine. He had a coolness about him, and I do believe it is a coolness that comes with age. He gave us a tour of his house, which was neat and charming, much like him.

I'm not as smooth as Rodrigo, and I don't glide like him, but I was comfortable around him, from the start.

'Your voice sounds like someone,' I told him.

He smiled, looking interested.

'Someone you know?'

'No, like, someone from the nineties.'

'Oh, God,' he said, still smiling

'I just watched a history on horror special, and like, maybe it's because I just watched it, but I think you may sound like Brandon Lee.'

Rodrigo furrowed his brows and laughed a little. He looked puzzled and entertained, a look from others that I am well-acquainted with. The familiarity of that feeling put me further at ease.

The three of us sat in Rodrigo's immaculate living room, complete with a Tom Bianchi coffee table book and a scented Home Goods candle, which smelled heavenly. There was polite conversation, about New York, about Covid, about what it's like to move out of the city. Nothing felt out of place, but there were small pauses after each of us spoke, signs that conversation was about to overstay its welcome. I saw the look in Rodrigo's eye, the look that we should proceed to the next step. Matthew sat in the chair next to him, being Matthew: nice, chill, cordial, the lovely Matthew-ish way of being.

'Should we move into another room?' I asked.

'We can stay here,' Rodrigo said, standing up.

He walked towards me, and I stood up too. He wrapped his mouth onto mine, opening it slightly, swirling his tongue. His body and its width felt good pressed against me. Matthew stood up, and the two of them kissed.

The three of us, naked from the waist down, took turns going down on each other. Rodrigo had mentioned before that he was a 'cocksucker,' although I didn't realize until now, how much he meant that. He was, by far, the best oral sex I've had. He was a combination of things that I found were what made Rodrigo... Rodrigo. He moved like an animal, as if he had not been nourished in days, weeks, months. Simply put, he was feeding. His head and neck bobbed feverishly up and down, and he hardly ever came up for breath. The only time he stopped and came up for air was when he would press his face against my balls, taking deep inhales.

'They smell so good,' he whispered.

That whisper, his sex voice was totally authentic. Most people, including myself, sound forced and odd when they sex-up their voice. Not Rodrigo. The sound of his voice was nothing short of an aphrodisiac. It was smooth, deep, and steady.

He and I began to go down on Matthew. While I sucked, Rodrigo whispered.

'Take that big cock. Share it with me.'

Then, I'd direct Matthew's dick into Rodrigo's mouth. Rodrigo kept eye contact with me while he sucked. One of his hands squeezed the bottom of my foot. He returned Matthew's dick to me, putting its head against my lips.

'Good boy,' he said.

He continued. 'Good boy. Suck your boyfriend's cock.'

'Husband's,' I said. A giant line of spit leaked out of my mouth as I corrected him.

Eventually, we moved from the couch to his bedroom. Rodrigo wasn't going to fuck me that night. What he wanted was oral and cum-filled. As we lay in his bed, I experienced a feeling of calm and ecstasy as Matthew and I were side by side and Rodrigo continued to take turns sucking us. At times, the three of us were all in each other's mouths, but this was Rodrigo's night, his night to feed.

'Are you getting close?' I asked Matthew, as Rodrigo lay on his stomach, giving him head.

'I'm close,' he said.

'Do you want us to cum now?' I asked.

Rodrigo stopped what he was doing and looked up at me. 'Are you timing it?'

'No, I just, I sort of have a talent. I can cum at any time. I can cum now, I can cum in twenty minutes. I can cum in an hour,' I said.

'It's true,' chimed in Matthew.

'Interesting,' Rodrigo said. 'I can start with him,' he said, meaning Matthew.

I watched him suck Matthew to completion. I'm not sure if Matthew had ever cum with me, just from head alone. He usually likes to finish himself off. But Rodrigo is a different kind of talent. I was smiling when I knew Matthew was cumming, when I knew his cum was going down Rodrigo's throat. Rodrigo swallowed, looking satisfied, leaned upward, and kissed me. He moved downward again, taking me into his mouth.

Usually I'm not the most vocal but tonight, I was inspired. 'Suck me, suck my dick. Fuck, yeah. Fuck, you feel so good.'

Rodrigo's mouth was going wild, his beard scratching against my inner thigh.

'I'm going to cum,' I said.

My legs spasmed as I shot into his mouth. The spasm started in my knees, went to my thighs, and shook my stomach.

For about a half-hour, Rodrigo laid between my legs, and the three of us talked. We talked about sex workers, Instagram thots, how kids are fucked up these days because their social skills are limited because their primary relationship is with their phone screen. Rodrigo did this thing: every few minutes he rubbed the bottom of his chin against my pubes. It reminded me of an animal, burrowing its head for comfort. And then, the room became so quiet, quieter than it already was. Rodrigo turned his face downward, and gently began to kiss my shaft. I was hard again, and he took me into his mouth. It's a moment that I didn't know I was craving. Rodrigo's warmth, that room, the pleasure I felt was woven with peace and contentment. Matthew next to me, watched as I came again in Rodrigo's mouth. The only sounds you could hear were my moaning, Rodrigo's spit, and the crickets outside. Afterward, the three of us lay there, in silence. Matthew's head was on my shoulder. Rodrigo lay on my chest. Gently, I rubbed the back of his head with the palm of my hand. Our breathing became more relaxed as we swayed in and out of sleep.

October 25

I'm not sure what it is but today is the first day since March that I haven't felt well. It could be the lingering effects of the Nyquil I took last night (to make myself fall and stay asleep). Maybe the sore throat I woke up to was on account of the temperature dropping last night and the heat in our building not kicking on. It felt like an icebox in our room this morning. Not long after we got up today, we walked down fourteen blocks to 59th St, to vote early for the election.

We got to the voting site 45 minutes before it opened, at 9:15 am. The line was already wrapped around the corner. The wait wasn't too terrible; we were headed back home by 10:45. The process of voting, during a pandemic, with people coming out in masses, was pretty organized. Inside the auditorium, it felt calm. People were alert, helpers were present, I didn't get any sense of confusion or aggravation from anyone. I think New Yorkers came in to do what they needed to do, and I was one of them. Maybe it was waiting in the cold that gave me a chill. I took my temperature and it was normal. I bought a jug of orange juice to keep hydrated with Vitamin C. I think I'll barricade myself in blankets tonight, put on a horror movie, and eat lollipops, drink more orange juice, and rest.

October 27

This pandemic and election has a way of keeping the things that I store in the back of my head, of coming to the forefront. Perhaps it's because if something remains unresolved, or unhealed, then conflict (which is broadcast 24/7) widens the wound. This morning, I thought of Florida, and how it's always been a swing state in presidential elections, and I pictured who it is that is voting red. And I thought about all of the older, rich, white men in Palm Beach who raised their golf-playing sons to be just like them. Those men, if you are not one of them, then they will see you as less, if at all. If you're Black, you're less. If you're gay, you're less. If you're a woman, you're less. I could always tell by the way they walk by you. They do not see you or your anger. There's nothing for them to feed off of, and if you have nothing to offer them, to give them, then you're not there.

Sometimes I don't know where the eyes and ears and heart and thought of Florida lies. I just had to explain to a family member that a SWAT Halloween costume isn't the most thoughtful costume to wear right now. There's this Florida bubble, at least among white people, and at least around white people who either have money or are receiving money from someone in a rich, white bubble; the bubble does not allow current events in: like systemic racism, police brutality, or a crooked administration, or even how dire a pandemic is. That's just all outside stuff in this crazy world, they may say.

It is the definition of apathy. Obviously, it's the same apathy that helps feed racism, a self-serving government, and the spreading of disease.

Not all Floridians are apathetic, by the way. The ones who are though, they seem to love boats. It seems like their happiness is whether or not they get to ride their boat down the intercoastal. Of course, riding a boat would not count for anything if you cannot show yourself riding on said boat. So, you must get selfies to post of yourself in a bathing suit, holding a handle of liquor, with your tongue out, partying on a boat, riding down the intercoastal during a pandemic, and hope that it doesn't get lost among what's trending right now: unarmed Black men being shot and killed by police.

While a 'nonpolitical' Floridian cruises down the coast, they may pass a few boats with Trump flags whipping in the wind. No one says anything out loud, or to each other. I mean, afterall, they just want to go out, have a little fun, drink a little, and to live a little today... and the next day... and the next day.

October 28, 1:17 pm

Maybe it's because of my and Matthew's night at Rodrigo's recently and the fact that our time spent there was comparable to Jonathan Harker at Dracula's castle, pinned down, falling into pleasure for as long as we could take, but I still feel pretty content. I'm not seeking more than what I have at this moment.

This morning, I walked to the Post Office and mailed two copies of *Curved*, the writing anthology I put together earlier this year, to readers in California and Colorado.

Matthew gave me a few copies of *Desirable Dudes*, his erotic male figure zine, to mail off as well. Every time I walk to the Post Office to mail something that is Queer, especially Queer writing, I think... this is all that I need, really, and I wish I could do it full time. To make a living full time, spreading Queer words. I guess that's the dream of many. As I was walking through my neighborhood, I was listening to the Mary Jane Girls and wearing a black leather jacket, and I wondered, would I be living this exact moment if it was 1985?

When my desire returns, which it will, it always does, and usually sooner than later, I wonder how I'll tend to it. Will I run past the black door on 19th Street, daring myself to go in? Do I glimpse inside adult video stores, especially the one on 3rd Avenue that keeps its doors open when the weather is pleasant? I may log on to Squirt again, and see what the cock-hungry kid from down the street is up to. I cannot help but ask, is this what it was like to be hungry in 1985? To be past the point of denying your desire toward other men, knowing the options of how to satisfy it, but be hesitant to do so because of a disease in the city that seeks to spread and replicate. It's too presumptuous of a question to ask, for me at least. We're not in that time and the people who were there, who are still here, that time is memorialized in their memory banks. It doesn't have a place for fantasy in mine.

4:06 pm

Rodrigo and I messaged each other, and we have something in common, maybe it's lust, or maybe his hunger is as strong as mine. As you can see, my contentment on a dreary afternoon didn't last long. He sent me a picture of his cock, and I was already stroking, so I showed him mine. He told me he wants to spend more time on my feet next time we're together. He said he doesn't care what we do, as long as we swap DNA.

Next time, I said, I want him to fuck me, with our mouths open, something I fantasized about when Matthew and I were there. 'I'm going to have to warm up to that, I've never bred with a boyfriend there.' Why he continues to call Matthew my boyfriend, I don't know. This fantasy, of him breeding me, while Matthew watches, was one of the first fantasies we shared, months ago. He had made it seem like this is something that he does or has done. Maybe he was just getting caught up in a fictional sex fantasy, and maybe he just went along with it because he didn't really think we'd meet. There's a chance, a very good chance, that he didn't think that I'd show up, with Matthew, to his house, in Woodstock, two hours outside of the city.

'I can tell that you're into me. And you know that I feel the same,' he wrote.

I paused for a moment. Even if he and I share a bond that is expressed through physical intimacy, a bond that I would treat with care, this isn't a love story (and not that he intends it to be) or one of biting into forbidden fruit.

My love story began six years ago, with Matthew, and it ebbs and flows, but it is ours and I may fuck it up once in a while, but I don't want anything to overshadow it. I don't really know what Rodrigo seeks anyway, as I'm not exactly sure of what I seek. I suppose that's what exploration is, the thing that I say I hunger for.

As he and I were messaging, I realized it was midday, and he was working from home.

'I'll let you get back to work, ' I wrote.

I threw my phone across the bed, and crept into sleep.

October 29

Back when there were races, pre-pandemic, Matthew and I would run half-marathons, maybe two or three a year. I didn't care how tired my legs and hips felt afterwards, it felt like my lungs and my stomach were cleared and renewed. Which, thinking back, especially since I was still smoking at the time, they probably were. The night before these races, you had to pick up your 'bib,' aka your racing number, and a complimentary T-shirt. The pick-up was usually at a pier in Brooklyn and they'd have hotdog vendors, and craft beer vendors, and Top-40 hits on loudspeakers playing. I mean, it's fucking corny, but Matthew always liked it as he gets pleasure from the little things. It was May 2016, and we were there, the night before the race, getting our bibs. I wasn't planning on drinking or staying long, but one beer with me, well, that's not enough.

Matthew and I had been together, at this point, for a year and a half. Being with Matthew has always felt natural, easy. We were, I guess, a sort of average, monogamous couple. An average, monogamous couple who took selfies together before we ran marathons. Look, I think people, in general, like Matthew and me. I don't think we've ever presented ourselves as bragging or showing off that we have something that others don't. That's not either one of our styles. At times, there may be a traditional element in how we present, but not in a heteronormative 'We're just like everyone else,' sort of way.

We had not yet had a threesome, or really, talked an extensive amount about sex or desire. We were, I don't want to say, becoming comfortable, but we were at the stage where we were becoming embedded in each other's lives, but not yet at the stage to discuss what that means if it's forever.

After we got our bibs, we ate some, probably took a picture of the sunset with Manhattan skyscrapers in the background. I had one beer, which turned into two, then three, I might have been on my fourth. The sun was setting, the temperature cooling, and I was drunk. I also had a pack of American Spirits in my bag, and thought, *I need a cigarette*. I was aware of how ridiculous it would look if I started smoking at a pre-marathon running rally, while drunk, which really is what made me want to do it. I still think it's pretty funny. It was also my 'fuck you' to all the sinewy, healthy runners around me. Fuck your craft beer, and your Top-40 music, and your casual stupid-ass discussions about how you're preparing for the race.

'Listen, I'm going to smoke a cigarette. I know it looks bad, I don't care. I'm going to lean over the railing over here,' I told Matthew.

'Okay,' he said, smiling a little.

Matthew and I were leaning over the railing, when two guys approached us. They had light hair, were muscular but not huge, and had Australian accents, like Chris Hemsworth but of average, human size.

'Can we borrow one of those from you?' one asked.

Happily, I handed them over two cigarettes and they lit up. The four of us were leaning over this metal railing, three of us smoking, ashing our cigarettes into the water.

'Do you know of any good pubs in the area we could go to at the end of the race?' they asked.

Matthew was sandwiched between us and rambled off a name or two. As our cigarettes waned, we made flighty plans to meet up after the race; plans that were forgotten as soon as we flicked our cigarette butts into the water. I wasn't aware of it then, but a switch in me had been flipped. After we left, Matthew and I went to a neighborhood bar, near my apartment, for 'one drink.' I remember when we got back to my place, Matthew flopped onto my mattress, which was on the floor, still with no bed frame after three years. It was 1 am. We had to be up in four hours to run thirteen miles.

I don't know why I did this, if it was intuition, as I had never done this before, but while Matthew slept, I walked across the room and went to his phone. There wasn't a lock on it, so I didn't have to put in a password or anything. I went to his Instagram app and went straight to his messages. His most recent messages, there had to be four or five of them, with different guys, were drenched in sex. They traded dick pics of each other. There were pictures of Matthew, showing off his cock and the bottom of his ass with messages like, 'Fuck me, I want your big cock in me.' My heart sank to the bottom of my stomach. I put the phone down, walked to my roommate's bedroom, who was still awake, and knocked on her door. I went inside, sat on her bed, put my head between my knees and started to hyperventilate.

'I am so stupid,' I said, over and over.

I woke Matthew up and told him what I found and told him to get out, which he did. It was almost 2 am. I didn't make it to the race in the morning. Matthew did, which, then I thought, how could he have it in him, after all of that to still run a marathon? Now, I think, maybe that's all he had, and he needed to do that, to accomplish something, to be okay.

For the next two weeks, we were still together but very apart. I barely spoke to him. I disabled Instagram. I was, in essence, a ghost. Matthew told me he would walk around the perimeter of Sunset Park, trying to think of ways to make it okay. After the initial hurt was over, I had to make peace with a few things, including things within myself.

Those guys, the Australian ones, they triggered something in me. There was an attraction on my end, perhaps on theirs, and with Matthew too. I didn't know what to make of it. I cannot control my attraction to other men, and I know that Matthew cannot either. And there's nothing I, or he, can do about that. So, what are we going to do?

One of the first things I did once we started speaking again was ask Matthew about his ex. I asked how often they had sex. I asked him how his ex was in bed. Did he do anything exceptionally well? I also knew that Matthew used to pose nude for photographers and sometimes he would jerk-off in front of them. I asked what he liked about it, what was it like jerking off on a couch while someone took your picture?

'It's like having sex with them, but you're not,' he said.

That answer intrigued me and still does. Is it the abstaining that gets him off? Is it voyeurism? Maybe it's both, I still don't know the answer. Matthew is like Pinocchio a little bit; lovable and evasive. They are both somewhat giddy, child-like; they are alive and want to love and have fun in the world. There's something there though, that you cannot quite get to. Would these boys ever willingly talk about themselves and their pasts if they weren't asked first? Or is that me projecting my own past and experiences, that I held so tightly?

When I got a sense of how strong Matthew's voyeurism was, I made a plan to play with it. I told him I wanted to make a porno, to film everything. I said, that I want to walk into his apartment and he'd be sitting there, watching men fuck on his TV. His cock would be out, and I'd walk in, bend down, start sucking him off. I even told him to wear his camouflage cargo shorts, which I saw as a jockish touch. I told him to have his phone ready, ready to film me and fuck me and film us doing it.

The day, leading up to that night, sex was all over my brain. I had that nervous, pent-up energy that I've grown accustomed to. That afternoon, I went for a run, before I went to Matthew's. I lived near Prospect Park, and would run the loop around the park, which is about three miles. I'm pretty sure I was listening to Madonna's *Erotica*. As I ran, I felt like eyes were on me, eyes of men. Their eyes were engaged with mine, for longer than what I was used to. Was I seeing this because of the sexed-up state I was in? I wasn't sure. I looked over to my left, and there was a man, Black, tall, thin, in his early twenties, standing on a shaded pathway that led into a bunch of trees. He stood there, looking at me. His eyes followed me as I ran. I didn't know it then, but he was inviting me to go with him.

October 30

Every Friday, there's this yoga person in Arizona, who I guess runs a hot, naked yoga session or studio, and asks his Instagram followers to submit a naked picture of themselves, if they want to, that is. He, of course, blurs out any genitalia. He does this, he says, as a way to promote body positivity. Normally, I wouldn't go for something like this, especially when there's a clause that says, 'Do Not Submit Thirst Traps.' Isn't everything a thirst trap?

I started submitting pictures, and I let this yoga person in charge blur me, and tag me too. When he uploads the pictures, he only posts them as stories, so they only stay up for 24 hours. We don't have mutual friends, so I don't worry about someone seeing the pictures who may not expect that of me. The first time I partook, I told Matthew about it. I didn't ask for permission, but it felt good to share. Today, I submitted a picture of me, with my face in it, my dick hard, the head right in front of the lens. I'm dripping wet, since I very carefully took the picture while showering.

Now, I guess this whole exercise is to raise body consciousness, but it's also a way to directly connect, and fast, with anyone who is into your picture. Within twenty minutes of the picture posted, you'll usually receive a few more followers and a couple DMs. To be honest, there is something freeing knowing that you're naked on the internet, and then something comforting in knowing that in 24 hours, you won't be. I think the approach of showing off your body, without shame, is honorable, but this is more of an exercise in desire, at least it becomes one for me. Today was no different, and coupled with the full moon that's expected tonight, maybe it felt more intense than usual.

Immediately, I had two guys not so subtly sneak into my DMs. One was named Tomás, who lived in El Salvador, and was 23 years old. His body was taut, his face smooth like a baby, with full, beautiful lips. His cock was thick, brown, and uncut. Photographers seemed to like him, as the majority of his pictures were of his shirtless body and professionally lit. His profile said he was an actor. The other guy, his name was Ryan. Ryan was Irish, or I think he was anyway. He was fair-skin, had thin lips, and blond-ish-red hair. He wore a lot of fitted, button-up shirts, and sensible business casual jeans.

'I loved your nude. We should fuck,' Ryan wrote.

I couldn't fuck Ryan, or Tomás for that matter, as they were in other countries. I did, however, start sexting with them at the same time. Ryan, he wanted to be fucked and have it rough. So, I gave him his fantasy. I told him I'd get his hole soft and wet for me. I'd push him onto the bed, put his arms over his head, and shove myself inside him. I told him it's going to hurt, which only excited him more. I said I'd choke him while I fucked him, with force. He didn't seem to mind the idea of pain, as he loved when I said my precum was mixing with the blood inside him. The bloody, semen-filled juice, I said, was leaking all over my thighs.

'Rape me,' he replied.

Now, let's be truthful. I've never had this kind of hard-core sex — well maybe once — but it was very late, after a bottle of whiskey, and I mainly just remember the guy worked for Bloomingdale's and had a Morrisey record propped up on display by itself, which I thought was incredibly tacky. Regardless, whoever this online Ryan person is, I was happy to get him off. But Tomás, Tomás presented something more to my liking. One of the first things he said was that he wanted for me to climb on his dick, and what a beautiful dick it was. I said I was going to put Tomás's arms behind his head (my thing) as I rode him. I wrote to Tomás that I wanted him to cum in me, and that's when he called me 'Daddy.'

'Do you want my cum, Daddy?'

'Yes, baby give Daddy your cum.'

'Do I make you happy, Daddy?'

I asked Tomás if he would be my boy, to which he agreed.

'Be a good boy and fill Daddy up,' I wrote.

Tomás said he wanted to fuck me so bad, that he would fuck me until I had a smile on my face. He asked if I was single, and I said no, I am married.

'Doesn't he mind, when I fuck his husband's ass?'

'No, no... in fact, I think he would prefer to watch.'

Tomás asked if Matthew and I could be his daddies, and I said yes, assuring him that he is our boy. That's when he asked to jerk off with me over cam, tonight. I said we could do that and I asked if he wanted Matthew to join.

'I just want to jerk with you first,' he said.

Matthew, who had no idea what had been happening with me in the bedroom over the course of the afternoon, had been painting in the living room and eating chocolate meant for Trick-or-Treaters. In true Matthew fashion, he did come in at some point, to give me hot dogs on wheat bread. He sliced them up, decorating them to look like bloody fingers, even indenting the skin on the hotdog where fingernails would be.

October 31

It's Halloween today, and there's a full moon tonight. Matthew and I couldn't find any pumpkins for sale, so we carved ones made of foam that he had gotten a couple of years ago at an arts and crafts store. His pumpkin is traditional, a replica of the one shown during the opening credits of *Halloween*. He even painted the edges of the foam orange, to make it look more realistic. My pumpkin has a gaping hole for a mouth. I carved triangular shapes on its sides, making it look like some kind of demonic stingray. Then I poured red paint into my hands, and smeared it all over, as if it had been bludgeoned. I found two cutting knives and stabbed them into its left and right sides. I think my pumpkin is what I feel when I know that I have to be patient. I have to be patient for time to pass, because the future will bring possibilities. With possibility comes exploration. New explorations may cause my cravings to subside, at least for a while. I'll have a little more contentment, in just a little bit of time.

NOVEMBER 2020

November 1, 12:47 am

I feel so trapped, as if I am stuck in a trap of blandness, where time is just passing by. I feel as though I am not growing, and I'm scared that Matthew is stuck, endlessly stuck in some sort of thick bog. Like he is underneath a film and is looking through it, and can see through the surface, but doesn't care and doesn't try to break through it. It's been a recurring fear that I've had about him for years, and I don't think it will go away. Sometimes, it feels like he is pre-programmed when moving about the day. He'll paint, cook dinner, even clean the dishes afterwards when I tell him not to and that I'll do them instead. He'll watch TV, fuck around on his phone, then at 11 pm will say 'I think I'm going to lie in bed.' The monotony is driving me insane. Where is the rush, what are the thoughts, the emotions?

I've asked him, 'Is anything wrong? Are you depressed?'

'No,' he says, with a surprised look on his face, everytime.

Sometimes, and more often than not as of late, I want to shake him, slap him alive in some ways, get him angry, get him sad, just get him to express something other than 'everything is okay and I'm fine'. I've known him for six years now and it's like I am still waiting to see what bubbles underneath his surface. Why am I not able to reach that spot? Where does that place exist in him and is it so buried that it is unrecognizable? There must be truths to him that he has not yet sought. Matthew sleeps very well in a bed of comfort and tradition, uninterrupted, while I stir and stir, my thoughts racing and digging, endlessly curious to see how far the ground below me goes.

8:29 am

I feel sad or desperate, as if I'm doomed to always be seeking. I know I'm not the only gay man that feels that way. It's this wandering life I guess, and no, a marriage certificate and financial security don't save you from that. The anxiety I felt last night before I went to sleep returned again this morning, as I sat there, on the couch, in silence, drinking coffee next to Matthew. I told him I was going to go into the other room to write. He said, 'I love you,' and kissed me on the lips.

9:08 am

If we're going to get Freudian right now, then, yes, I fear that a complacent life will strip myself of sex and exploration. Except, it's not all about sex, or maybe it is if we're talking Freud. It's also about domesticity, and I wonder if a domestic life threatens to rob one of their innate desires. While I could say that I don't think that gay men are necessarily programmed to be domestic, it is I who I fear may not be programmed for it. I feel too wild and I question if Matthew understands that feeling. Sometimes I don't know if I have anyone to relate to, especially now, especially since being quarantined together for eight months, every day being a routine. I never cared for schedules, or fixed meals, or going to bed at the same time every night, or having received 1,000 'I love yous' throughout the day, which is what I have now. Fuck, I see myself writing that and I think, how can you write that, especially when it could be that love and structure that helps ground you? How can you say that when you have someone who does so much for you, every day – someone whose happiness depends on your own. Perhaps it is that responsibility, the fact that someone's happiness depends on my own that makes me feel like being safe is being in a cage. And when I feel caged, I feel sad for feeling that way. A friend of mine snapped at me, a few weeks ago, and said that she felt that I showed a 'lack of humiliation' for my home. I didn't agree with her, and I appreciate all of what I have, and maybe appreciating it is what makes me feel guilt or sadness, or I'm not sure exactly what. I feel alone right now, like a feral cat inside a house, staring at the porch door, wanting to go back outside, but the door is closed.

Eventually, I'll calm down. There's a large part of me that has surrendered to the fact that I will continue, at times, to feel trapped. Whether it's anxiety, my gut, or a franticness, an energy that is too strong that I do not know what to do with, I don't know if any of that reasoning matters. What I do know is this – when my anxiety starts recurring at the rate that it does, and when it involves Matthew and me, there is a reason why it keeps coming back. I fear complacency and I need to talk about that fear with him and most of the time, there is not much of a conversation that takes place. Matthew may be unsure how to navigate these things. He could be fearful of making me mad. He may not even feel that there is a problem and it is me who comes off as alien. So, I start to feel alone and that's when I'm struck by the fear that nothing will change. He watches me when that fear takes over and I start to go in circles. I want him to be able to talk with me and to talk about us so that I can get out of this circular path where I start repeating my words, and I go so far into myself that it feels like there is no way out. Matthew watches when this happens, with a helpless look in his eye.

Slightly bowing his head, he says, 'I'm sorry you're sad.'

3:35 pm

While I analyze myself, it looks like Leo, in New Paltz, may be having his own existential crisis. Two weeks have passed since he told me that he didn't want to be involved with anyone in an open relationship and that, I don't know, we should detach a little, or maybe I shouldn't visit him anymore. Today, he gave me an offer. He sent me a text saying that he was inviting myself and Matthew, and another friend of ours in an open relationship, and maybe two or three local boys to spend three days in a cabin together in January.

As favorable as that sounds, I couldn't deal with the contradiction of it all. Didn't he just say that he did not want to spend his time with men in open relationships? I asked him about it and I told him that when compared to the text that he sent me, where he was seemingly pushing me away, this presented itself as confusing. He explained himself, or tried to. He told me that after I'd left his place, after spending a weekend with him, that he became sad. He said he thought he should instead be focusing his time on finding and building a relationship like Matthew and I have. I understand that and I did think about how when I left New Paltz, and returned home to Matthew, that he would be alone that night. I thought the same thing about Matthew, when I was with Leo. That he was sleeping alone. In theory, I was the one getting the best of both worlds.

I told Leo that I needed a little bit of time to process.

'If it's alright, I just need a reset,' I texted.

Leo said he hopes for the two of us to be on the same page, whatever page that is. Ten minutes later, I received a text:

'Let me know if there is anything I can do to help you reset. If you need me to push a reset button, or to blow one...'

I didn't respond. What he doesn't see is that aside from my aggravation, the edge of my lip slightly, very slightly, lifted into a smile of disdain.

Leo acts like a troublemaker, and while I may not fall for his antics, I know his heart is good, and his confusion of what to do and how to seek what he needs is real. His mischievousness is not vicious. Like a boy on a playground, he wants to see if one will chase him after he pushes you a little too hard during a game of tag. When he runs away, he'll turn around to see if you're there. He knows I'll be there, smirking at him, a look of warning in my eye.

November 2

It's difficult today to formulate thoughts and put them down, or try to present them objectively. It's the evening before the election. Over the weekend, there were Trump supporters blocking the Mario Cuomo bridge, apparently attempting to run a Biden campaign bus off the road, and Trump just tweeted that under a Joe Biden presidency, the country will go into a prison state and you won't be able to celebrate Christmas. People are stocking up on food for the next week and businesses are boarding their windows.

It's the sort of thing where there's a bit of a loss for words. I made a mental checklist in the shower of if Matthew and I have what we need. He went food shopping this morning, and maybe I'll pick up some additional water at the bodega. Why are we planning for a natural disaster or some sort of coup? I thought about what we each have in our bank accounts, if we're insured, and the fact that my New York State ID is valid for Canadian travel. It's like I'm prepping for *Handmaid's Tale* or to be Linda Hamilton when SkyNet takes over. There is, however, a collective intensity that's vibrating throughout the country right now, and it's not even the day of the election. I'm going to watch Election Night coverage, obviously, but maybe I'll watch a movie or something during the day instead of endless election news. We'll see if I have that kind of self-discipline.

November 3, 12:13 pm

I woke up at about 5 am today and my first thought was, okay, I got about five hours sleep, which for me is about average or just slightly below. Not bad for the night before the election. Somehow I managed to fall back to sleep, although not very deeply, for about another hour.

It's barely past noon right now and it's just going to be a day of waiting. The headlines in the newspaper talk about anxiety being high, people's social media posts are about methods and suggestions of how to de-stress during Election Day. This looming feeling of what is going to happen is not going anywhere for the next few hours, or days even, and it makes time move slowly.

10:38 pm

Watching the election coverage has become depressing. Even if Joe Biden were to win, which at the current moment, it looks like he is not, half of the country that voted is in favor of Donald Trump. At this point, 'Fuck America' is the slogan that should be used nationwide. I've never been patriotic, but it is so backwards here, and has been for so long that maybe the only focus that matters is community focus and what you can do for others. I would say that if Trump wins, America has fallen, but fallen from what exactly? What pedestal was it even on to begin with? The only lesson I'm seeing in this, especially if Trump wins, is to look out for others and for your loved ones. To care and advocate for them the best way you can.

November 4, 6:15 am

A Presidential winner has still not been announced and may not even be announced today. Before I went to bed last night, I posted that regardless of who wins, America has shown itself. America has always been a country deeply rooted in racism. What we're seeing now, is the death grasp that it continues to have in order to maintain the reign of white supremacy. At this point, this isn't a nail-biter where I'm going to tune into CNN to see who wins. America is just continuing to let us see what it is: a country so terrified of losing it's white privilege that even death, illness, and murder are not strong enough to constitute change.

November 5, 7:23 am

I know at least half of the country feels this way, but I don't think I can be fully present until Biden is declared President Elect. Even if I were to read, or watch a movie, or jerk-off, it would just be a distraction from following the voting count. I didn't even cum last night in the shower, and I'm not totally sure why. It might have been because this counting process of the votes is like an intense session of edging. It just keeps going and going. It only seemed appropriate to not let out a release because I won't mentally feel a release until I know Trump is defeated. It's strange isn't it? In a way, Joe Biden is holding my cum hostage.

Matthew's not letting it get to him. Yesterday, I was in the bedroom, and I walked out quickly and quietly. When I rounded the corner and got to the living room, Matthew turned around looking surprised, as if he was caught. I looked down and he was adjusting his pants and threw a small yellow towel to the floor.

'Were you jerking off? I asked.

'Yeah, I thought you were sleeping.'

2:44 pm

The news is reporting that Biden could claim the Presidency tonight. Pennsylvania could be the state that decides the election. I hope that there will be a collective sigh of relief. Of course, it won't be felt by all Americans, especially the ones who made the choice that their comforts were more important than the civil rights of their Black, Brown, Queer, undocumented, and underappreciated fellow Americans. There's a lot of people though, including myself, that have been waiting for the day that Donald Trump is defeated. I want to see the headlines that will be splashed over publications worldwide come tomorrow morning.

7:47 pm

Soon it won't be enough to just complain about Donald Trump. Complacency will invite itself in, once again. It'll tempt you to nap and while you rest, white patriarchy will watch over you, like a parent admiring their child's peaceful sleep.

November 7

When I was ninteen and a freshman in college, I would hang out in a friend's dorm and there was this guy, Mike, that I went to high school with. Because the dorm rooms were so small, the side- by-side beds were practically touching each other. Mike would lay on the edge of one bed, and I would lay on the edge of the other. With his body close to me, my entire left side was vibrating. I was having a body high, as long as he laid there, next to me. Whether he felt it or not, I don't know, but it felt like our energies were spilling out, meeting, mingling, and dry-humping each other.

I don't think I'm opposed to thinking of myself as a light masochist because strain, really, is my pleasure. I used to try to ignore the ache, numb it with denial. The ache's strength would always win, so I've had to make peace that I sometimes like and often hate just a little bit of pain.

I've even come to experience some satisfaction in how the election is going, which is ongoing, torturous, and pleasurable. Every hour, just a few more thousand votes for Biden come in, gently chipping away at Donald Trump's path to re-election. We already know that he cannot win, but the media will not call a winner, not yet, not while the votes are still being tallied. So, we just wait, for hours and hours, while we see the hole of Trump's defeat becoming deeper and deeper.

12:05 pm

Joe Biden has been announced as the next President-Elect. I was standing in the living room, still in my bathrobe, when I saw 'PROJECTION' sprawled across the television screen.

'It's happening,' I said.

Matthew looked over, not sure of what I was talking about.

'They're calling it. Right now, they're calling it.'

'Joe Biden is now President-Elect of the United States,' said Wolf-Blitzer.

I heard a man yelling, 'We won' on the street outside of our building.

There have been videos of people cheering and dancing in the streets. Horns were honking for minutes on end. CNN co-host Vann Jones wept on air, saying that Americans can finally take a breath. I texted my closest friends and spoke to my mother, who all said, 'It's finally over'. Sometimes, I suspect that if one puts in the work and effort and demands for a better outcome, a change can occur. If enough people stand up and try, it can be delivered. There's still so much to do, and the fact that 70 million Americans voted for Donald Trump, well, change isn't guaranteed. It never is and no matter what, it's never easy.

6:11 pm

I ran to the park today and I looked out onto the field, which was filled with people. Some of them were even dancing. I stopped to take a picture, especially since the sun seemed extra golden. As I was framing the shot, a series of claps started on one side of the park. The applause moved like a wave. Suddenly, the people around me were clapping. I tucked my phone underneath my arm and clapped with them. The clapping spread throughout the whole field, ending in cheers and sounds of celebration.

November 8

Mary MacLane wrote about Nothingness, and about waiting for happiness to come. I'd imagine that looking out at her town, Butte, Montana, she saw nothing for herself, as a nineteen-year-old Queer-esque woman. She belonged to her isolation, which she documented, and then shared for the world to see. As I've said, my angst is not more important than another's pain, nor my experiences more poignant than another's.

But I know what it's like to feel like someone is pressing their hand against my mouth, when there is no one there. To want to be alone, in a room, in my own thoughts, falling, instead of engaging with the one I love. To yearn for pleasure, to know that it's there, all around me, but I cannot have it when I crave it most. To always feel like I'm waiting, and time passes by, and I'm still waiting. Life though, is happening while I wait, and I fear that I may not be feeling as much as I could or should because of a bottomless pit of want inside me.

That is only a fear though, and fear comes and goes.

The difference between my present as opposed to my past, is that I'm not shutting everything down when dread seeps in. Dread and me kind of go together, it's like a slow fog that enters under the crack of a door. Now though, instead of suffocating, I'll just open the door of the fog-filled room and let the dread pour out and dissipate. I've spent a lot of time feeling alone, not wanting to belong to something larger. I am a part of something larger, whether I like it or not; a society that I contribute to, whether I think I'm a part of it or not. And time keeps going, and I keep aging. The world isn't what it was ten years ago, and neither am I. I think, at least at this moment, that I can navigate it more smoothly because I can travel within myself now, with much more ease.

November 9

It's about 9 am and the sun is bright, with a mist in the air. The leaves on the trees in Greenwood Cemetery, where I sit, are orange, and red, yellow and green. Flocks of geese are talking to each other while flying across a pond. It is a picturesque fall day with temperatures like its early summer, reaching up to 70 degrees. Ripples in the water cast shadows on tips of grass and on the limbs of trees.

I don't know what's going to happen in the future or where I'll land. I know that Matthew will be here, as he always is, by my side. That's not something I take for granted. Sometimes, I remember what it was like to be in bed with him years ago, his arm around me and I said, "You make me feel safe." While at times I need that moment, I choose not to live off of it for too long. He and I are a part of whatever the future is going to be and while I feel unsure of so much, I know we have to adapt and we have to change with it. What I'm saying is: I no longer want the crutch of relying on past narratives. I cannot rely on their safety. With everything that's happened this year, there's been a breakage of the norm, and what we tell ourselves, and I need to figure out what to move towards. Perhaps, something new to live by.

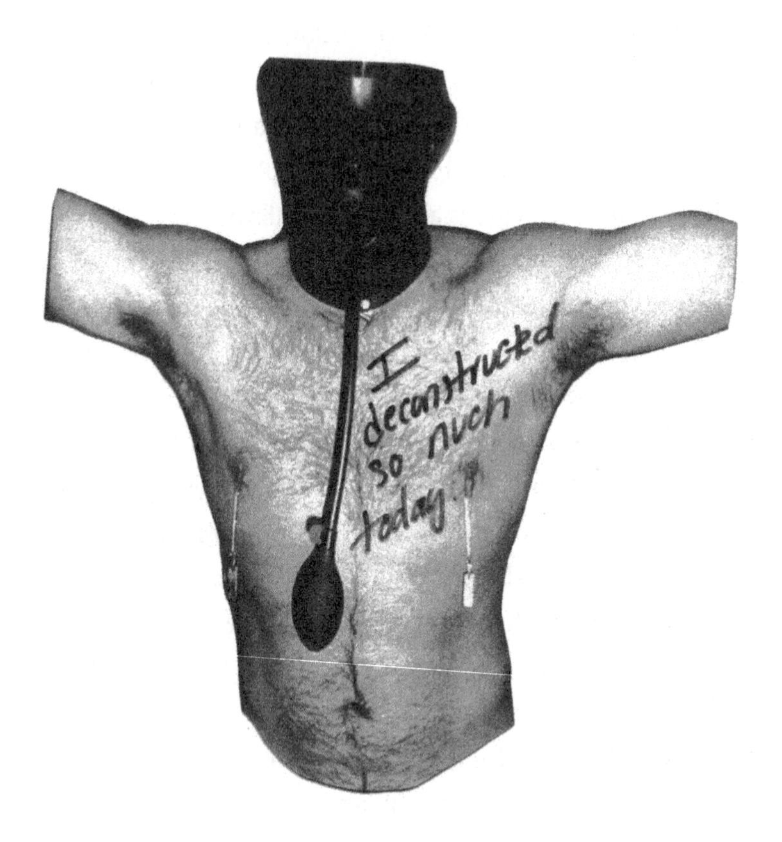
I
deconstructed
so much
today.

POST

April 20, 2021

Today I was walking down 5th Avenue in Brooklyn and I thought of how Mary MacLane wrote an envoi or *L'Envoi*, a summarization of her Portrayal, six months after her last written entry. She said that her book, *I Await the Devil's Coming*, was all she had and she wondered how, if released, it would be received.

> *Will the wise wide world itself give me in my outstretched hand a stone —*

I asked myself, what could I say that I have not already shared in my 90 days of writing? The first thing that came to mind was that shortly after my last entry in November, my mom suffered a heart attack. She lives alone and called the ambulance herself and spent nearly a week in the hospital. I flew down to Florida the day she was released. That night, as I was washing my face before bed, I heard a loud thud come from her bedroom. I knew it was her. When I opened the door, she lay flat on the ground, her head tilted at the bottom edge of her dresser. She could hardly speak, was barely conscious, her nightgown crumpled. I called 911, my adrenalin spiking, like it wanted to come out of me. I was moving so fast that to speak in cohesive sentences took effort. I shoved aspirin in her mouth and poured a glass of water through her lips as I spoke to the operator. She was taken to the hospital and it seemed as though her lungs had collected fluid and a high dosage of her blood pressure medication caused her to fall and pass out. She got to the hospital and made it out okay, and it has urged me to write what I already know; that what we're experiencing right now, as I write this, as you read this, what we know of ourselves and of others, it will come to an end.

During my walk today, I passed my friend Nydia's neighborhood and thought I'd pick up a snack for her, as she works all day teaching at a prestigious NYC art school via Zoom and sometimes forgets to eat. I said I'd drop off a bagel and coffee outside her front door. I had Nydia's keys (I lived with her when I met Matthew) and I let myself into her building, balancing a tray of coffee and bagels. I heard her inside, teaching her class remotely, and instead of dropping the food off at the door, I decided to make myself comfortable and took a seat in her backyard (that you can access through the hall), drank my coffee, ate my bagel, and watched on my phone as the jury was about to announce the verdict of the Derek Chauvin murder trial on CNN. I texted her that I was in her yard, which I think both scared and amused her.

After Nydia finished her lesson and found me outside eating a bagel, we went in and I listened to her speak about the know-it-all yet inquisitive and questioning nature of many of her students. She showed me a list of their complaints about a lack of diversity in their curriculum (which she agreed with) and promised she would talk to the staff and advocate for them, which I know she will. We turned on CNN, the verdict was read, guilty for all three counts, including second and third degree murder. A journalist held a microphone up to a little Black girl outside the courthouse and asked if she knew why the crowds were celebratory. In a soft voice, she answered 'I don't know' and turned inward, shying away from the camera. Her innocence, at that moment, a precious thing, it too will end.

Mary MacLane said that her book, her Portrayal, was the only thing that was important to her and the only thing that mattered. We all want to be seen and we make sure that we are: through our art, our social media posts, our comments, our stories, pictures and poses. And every day we start it all over again; a chance to be seen, or lauded, or commented on, or criticized or just acknowledged. What happens if that isn't enough: when you realize that your experiences are finite; that your time is finite; that your mother is finite; that that little girl in front of the courthouse is finite; that this print is finite? It is impossible to exist forever, to not be forgotten, but I suppose that the impossible is why we try.

Content warnings Substance abuse, race relations, mental health, body image, mention of rape/violent sexual fantasies.

Content within *Harsh Cravings* touches upon sensitive subjects and the controversial. It is the intent of the author and publisher to present a work which provides a freedom of expression that is both reflective and cognizant of any triggering or traumatic responses that it may present to its readers.

This information is given in hope that it will enable readers to protect themselves from harm, but we accept it is not exhaustive and may not include all issues that could affect people. If you have suggestions of how this can be improved, or additional warnings you feel should be included, and feel able to reach out, please contact us and we will try and accommodate as much as we can in future publications we release.